HAWAIIAN
LEGENDS OF GHOSTS
and
GHOST-GODS

HAWAIIAN
LEGENDS OF GHOSTS
and
GHOST-GODS

collected and translated from the Hawaiian

BY

W. D. WESTERVELT

with an Introduction by Glen Grant

Mutual Publishing

ISBN 1-56647-076-5

Cover illustration by Brian Ibaan
Cover design by Jane Hopkins

First Printing, February 1999
1 2 3 4 5 6 7 8 9

Mutual Publishing
1215 Center Street, Suite 210
Honolulu, Hawaii 96816
Telephone (808) 732-1709
Fax (808) 734-4094
e-mail: mutual@lava.net
url: http://www.pete.com/mutual

Printed in Australia

CONTENTS

FOREWORD

The advancement of a people is profoundly influenced by three factors, namely: the source and quality of their food supply; their contacts and associations with other peoples; and their religious beliefs and activities.

It is, perhaps, the last factor that influences people most in matters respecting their intellectual development, especially when these beliefs and activities are laid out along rational lines. As intelligence increases, knowledge is gained concerning the various phenomena of life and the relation that man bears to the forces of nature that have an influence over him. Until such a state of intelligence is attained, the developing race conceives for itself gods, ghosts, and other supernatural forms to give it the connected relations between itself and the things and phenomena of nature which cannot be understood. Through the instrumentality of these supernatural forms, the imagination of a people is developed. Songs and legends originate, blending accounts of the lives and exploits of the living and dead with those of the supernatural beings, and in time these form literature and develop arts of great value to the people.

The ethnology of the peoples of the Pacific is an interesting and profitable field for study, and especially is this true of the Hawaiians, for during the period within the knowledge of man they have shown capacity for rapid intellectual development. In the dawn of their history they had no written language, but they were rich in songs and legends, not only of their own exploits, but also of their relations with the superior influences that guided their destinies. These were repeated at fireside and feast, until the imagination of the people became directive and resourceful. So there should be little wonder that they learned readily and that their transformation under organized government and institutions was rapid.

The chapters that follow are replete with the richness of the imagery peculiar to the Polynesian, and no doubt none will appreciate this volume of legends more than the people of Hawaii themselves. May it serve them as a light showing the path they have trod in passing through the valley of superstition to the high lands of truth and understanding.

The author is to be congratulated because of the patience and persistence with which he has worked in this little-known field of ethnology and also for the clearness and completeness of his narrative. As this part of the world comes into the full measure of its importance may this book of "Legends of Ghosts and Ghost-gods" win wide appreciation as a contribution to our knowledge of the Pacific Islands.

J. W. GILMORE,
Professor of Agronomy,
University of California

BERKELEY, CAL.
October, 1916.

HAWAI'I'S SACRED NARRATIVES
AN INTRODUCTION

by Glen Grant

Ku'ilioloa *heiau* is an ancient Hawaiian temple situated on Kane'ilio Point at Poka'i Bay in the Wai'anae district of O'ahu. Although the site was destroyed by the United States military during World War II for the construction of an observation bunker, the three platforms of the sacred edifice have been partially restored, the grounds landscaped with *hala* and banana trees. The vistas on all sides of Ku'ilioloa are stunning, encompassing deep-blue Pacific waters rimmed by the towering peaks of the ancient Wai'anae volcano and the sweeping, yellow and green-tinged valleys that gently slope to white sand beaches.

To the south of Ku'ilioloa stands Pu'u o Hulu, named for a chief who was once in love with Ma'ili'ili, one of twin sisters whom he could not tell apart. Frustrated at the chief's inability to determine which of the two sisters he loved, a *mo'o* (supernatural lizard) changed the sisters and the chief into mountains. Frozen eternally into stone, he gazes longingly upon the twins, trying to discern which of the two mountains—Pu'u Ma'ili'ili or Pu'u Paheehee—he loves.

Visible also from Kuʻilioloa is the rounded top of Puʻukaʻala, the tallest mountain on Oʻahu, and Puʻukawiwi, believed to have once been a *puʻuhonua* (place of refuge) during war. To the north is Maunalahilahi, or the "thin mountain" that overlooks the famous surfing point at Makaha beach. Steeped in the history and lore of *ka poʻe kahiko* (the people of old), the powerful images of the Waiʻanae coast from this ancient temple can transport the viewer across the barriers of time, change and culture to a psychological realm where physical reality blends with the sacred narratives, illuminating a worldview rooted in the universal cosmology of the human past.

Papakala, the long-time *kahu* (guardian) of Kuʻilioloa, instinctively understood these mythological linkages between the past and present when he helped transport a small group of Honolulu senior citizens several hundred years into the past with his skillful storytelling. Taking an historical tour of Waiʻanae during the summer of 1987, the group stumbled onto Papakala, an elderly *kamaʻaina* (long-term resident of the area), who was diligently planting the small stalks of banana and *hala,* which a few years later would blossom into the rich vegetation adorning the temple. Although he had no idea what the group was doing in Waiʻanae, he graciously served as a host to Kuʻilioloa, openly sharing his knowledge of the *moʻolelo* (history) and *kaʻao* (tales) of the sacred site he lovingly tended. He explained how the temple was named for the legendary dog who was the protector of travelers. "Long dog Ku" was the literal English translation for this mythical beast who once battled and was defeated by the famous pig demigod, Kamapua'a.

Although often associated with the wetter, windward shores of O'ahu in the valleys of Kahana and Kaliuwa'a, Kamapua'a also lived for a time on the slopes of Pu'uka'ala with his grandmother, Kamaunuaniho. In the night he would forage in the taro *lo'i* (terraces) of the Wai'anae farmers, stealing taro and destroying the patches. Recognizing that a pig had done this damage, the farmers laid a trap for the nocturnal thief and finally caught Kamapua'a, whom they took to Pu'ukahea to bake in an *imu* (underground oven). The men tied the pig to the rock Pahoa and began to prepare the oven, when the many supernatural forms of Kamapua'a marched across the plains of Wai'anae, catching his captors and devouring them. Only those who managed to flee survived the wrath of Kamapua'a, and the Pahoa stone thereafter became associated with the demigod.

Another ancient god associated with Wai'anae, according to Papakala, was Maui-a-Kalana, the great trickster god of the Pacific. Born at Ulehawa on the south side of Wai'anae, Maui engaged in many of his famous exploits in this district of O'ahu. According to one sacred narrative, Maui was living seaward of Ulehawa when he saw two women, 'Alaenuiahina and 'Alaehuapipi, toasting bananas in the valley of Pohoa'alae. These women were supernatural beings who possessed *ahi Pele* (the fire of Pele). Swiftly descending upon them, Maui grabbed 'Alaehuapipi by the head, saying, "Show me how fire is obtained or I will kill you." To save her life, the secret of making fire was given to Maui, who then revealed to human beings how sparks were created when two sticks were rubbed together.

On another occasion, Maui's mother, Hina, was having difficulty properly drying her tapa because the sun was moving too fast through the sky. Maui climbed one of the mountains in Waiʻanae, where he caught the sun's rays, forever slowing its path through the Hawaiian skies. The stone anvil of Hina, the cave where she made her tapa and the mountain upon which Maui stood, Heleakala (literally, "snare by the sun"), are all found today in Waiʻanae. Although a popular version of this tale places Maui at Haleakala on the island of Maui, at Waiʻanae the ancient legends persist that those mythical events took place on the leeward coast of Oʻahu.

When Papakala finished mesmerizing the group with his stories of old Waiʻanae, he was asked whether the temple at Kuʻilioloa was still used for religious purposes. Yes, he answered, for all the four major *akua* (gods) of Hawaiʻi were embodied within this temple. One of the few temples in Hawaiʻi surrounded on three sides by water, the *heiau* was a place of worship for the god Kanaloa, whose domain was the sea. Above Kuʻilioloa was the domain of the god Lono, the expansive blue sky which seems to envelop the temple as completely as the sea. In the evenings, the *heiau* was used to study the stars in connection with navigation. Named for the god Ku, the temple was situated on the point named for the god Kane. Leading us from one corner of the top platform to the next, Papakala intimated that "Here

I worship Lono; here I worship Ku, here I worship Kane and here I worship Kanaloa." Perhaps concerned that there were Christians among the group who would be offended by his open faith in the ancient religion and worship of the four great *akua*, he concluded his tour by guiding the group to the center of the *heiau*. "Here," he proudly said, "I worship Iesu Kristo."

There was a venerable quality to the weathered, old face of Papakala that beamed that day in Wai'anae, proudly sharing the traditions of his temple with these strangers from Honolulu. Age had whitened his closely cropped hair and removed most of his teeth, leaving a mumbling quality to his rich baritone voice, which frequently intoned his native language. It was impossible to measure the number of years this *kama'aina* had lived on earth, but his deep-brown eyes looked through hundreds of years of the past. Like the beaten-down temple that he had helped restore and cared for, there was a spiritual resilience within Papakala that transmuted the motorized skiffs churning past in Poka'i Bay, the occasional jet aircraft overhead or the distant roar of motors along busy Farrington Highway. In his sacred narratives, this humble person left with these Honolulu *malihini* (visitors) a lasting truth: "*Ua lehulehu a manomano ka 'ikena a ka Hawai'i* ("Great and numerous is the knowledge of the Hawaiians").

Papakala is no longer physically among the living, but remains as a spirit of the native civilization that empowers Wai'anae with a special *mana* (divine power). Although often disparaged and ridiculed as a district with many social problems, Wai'anae remains an overwhelmingly Hawaiian place that, despite stereotypes and socio-economic challenges, breathes the cultural values of *aloha kanaka* and *aloha 'aina* (love of human beings and land) inherited through the centuries. Of course, the *malihini* from outside Wai'anae who ventures into the district without the insight of a *kama'aina* may be blind to the sense of place. Without a knowledge of Hawaiian place names, the history, legends and sacred sites, Wai'anae is simply another rural area impacted by sprawling shopping centers, increased traffic, crowded housing and more and more concrete. Without the guidance of a Papakala who can transform a rock or hill into sacred mythology, any place in Hawai'i remains just pretty scenery devoid of substance, a massive Hollywood backdrop useful for a *Jurassic Park* of computerized dinosaurs but lacking the Hawaiianness that provides residents or visitors with a depth of knowledge and understanding.

The sacred and profane narratives of Hawai'i, the mythologies, legends and folk tales of the ancient people who bequeathed a treasure house of knowledge to the present generations remain largely inaccessible to the modern *malihini* (whether born and raised in the islands or not) who daily pass by sites or places totally lost to them in time. Not having the advantage of a Papakala to personally share the stories of the past, the modern island *malihini* has no idea that the dramatic peak of Olomana was once a giant thief, slain Goliath-like by a young chief from Kaua'i, or that the so-called "Chinaman's Hat" (a name that should be forever erased from this historic isle) is the tail of Mokoli'i, a *mo'o* killed by Hi'iaka, the sister of Pele. The old axiom that "truth is stranger than fiction" holds especially true in terms of the legendary places of Hawai'i—the reclaiming of the ancient mythologies and place names in modern Hawai'i will provide a far more compelling and dramatic understanding of the islands' past than the current crop of superficial names such as "Crouching Lion," "Round Top," "Punchbowl," "Diamond Head," "Yokohama Bay" or "Tantalus" on O'ahu, or "Rainbow Falls" and "Paradise Park" on Hawai'i. While the modern English names may have a colorful story behind them, they are in no way as interesting or as insightful as the Hawaiian names they eventually replaced.

The only way to reconnect with the islands' Hawaiian sense of place, in lieu of obtaining one's own personal storyteller, is through the written records made available through the efforts of several nineteenth-century collectors of the oral traditions of *mo'olelo* and *ka'ao*. Fortunately for the modern reader, among these collectors were a few Hawaiian historians, such as David Malo and Samuel M. Kamakau, who recorded the myths and legends of native people whose lives bridged the eighteenth and nineteenth centuries. Published in the Hawaiian-language newspapers of the day, these rich sources of history preserved for posterity the legends of chiefs great and small, the sacred mythologies of gods and ghost-gods, the infamous battles and rivalries, the folk tales and daily lore of the *maka'ainana* (the people) and the reasons behind the naming of the places, stones, beaches and valleys of the islands. Included among the Hawaiian collectors of lore should be King Kalakaua, whose *Myths and Legends of Hawai'i* added many family traditions to the recorded legends of old.

Even as the *haole* (Caucasian) presence in nineteenth-century Hawai'i radically transformed the biological, economic, land, political and legal systems of the islands, leading to the destruction, disenfranchisement and dislocation of the native people, several foreign scholars in the islands began to record the ancient native myths and legends for an English-speaking audience. With the popularity of the Grimm brothers' first collection of "fairy tales," European and American scholars during the second half of the nineteenth century began earnestly collecting the "folklore" of ethnic groups throughout the world. In Hawai'i, this effort to record Hawaiian lore may have been in part motivated by the paternalistic belief that, since the native race was seen as "passing from the scene," the nostalgic remembrance of folk materials would preserve memories of a people whose physical presence had perished under the advancement of Anglo-Saxon civilization.

One of the earliest foreign scholars of Hawaiian folklore was Abraham Fornander, a former student of a Swedish rectory preparing for the ministry who abandoned religion for life on a whaling ship. After deserting the life of the sea in 1844 at Honolulu, Fornander settled in the islands, becoming over the years a coffee planter, surveyor, newspaper editor, inspector of the schools and a judge. Married to a Hawaiian woman, he was actively involved in native affairs, working with young men such as Malo and Kamakau to collect the lore and history of the native people. His publications *An Account of the Polynesian Race* and *Collection of Hawaiian Antiquities and Folklore* are among the most important and accurate histories written in the nineteenth century. Fornander's collection of folklore is still a vital resource for anyone interested in studying Hawaiian mythology and is suggested to even the most casual reader of island folk tales or history.

Among the more literary renditions of Hawaiian folklore were the publications of Thomas Thrum and William Drake Westervelt, whose works remain the most widely read and reprinted English versions of ancient myths and legends.

William Drake Westervelt drew upon the collections of Malo, Kamakau, and Fornander to popularize Hawaiian folklore through such widely read volumes as *Legends of Maui* (1910), *Legends of Old Honolulu* (1915), *Legends of Gods and Ghost-Gods* (1915), *Hawaiian Legends of Volcanoes* (1916) and *Hawaiian Historical Legends* (1923). Westervelt obtained his A.B.A. and B.D. degrees at Oberlin College in Oberlin, Ohio, where he was born. Pastor of churches in Cleveland, Ohio and Colorado, he settled in the islands in 1899, marrying missionary descendant Caroline D. Castle. As a member of the Hawaiian Board of Missions, he was active in developing a multicultural religious community, serving as superintendent of the Sunday School of the Portuguese Church and giving generously in time and money to the Japanese Christian churches, including Makiki Christian Church and the Korean Christian Institute. Westervelt's interest in Hawaiian lore, customs, beliefs and history was an avocation that led to numerous magazine and newspaper articles which were reprinted in his several collections. When he passed away at his Waikiki home in 1939, he was widely eulogized as Hawai'i's foremost authority on the folklore of the islands.

While this anthology of Hawaiian myths, legends and folk tales represents the very best of the English versions of an Hawaiian view of the sacred and profane, the tales have been filtered through the pen of outsiders who often embellished, altered or even censored the original materials that they drew from native sources. Though the gist of the tale may be authentic, the modern reader should be cognizant that much of the Hawaiian lifestyles, beliefs and even "earthy" or "bawdy" elements reflected in the stories have been altered or removed. In an effort to present the lore of ancient Hawai'i to a modern Victorian or Edwardian audience, it was sometimes necessary to introduce into the story such Christian notions as monogamous marriages so as not to offend the sensibilities of the prudish reader. One can only conjecture (not without a smile) the discomfort these haole writers must have felt when they attempted to present an Hawaiian tale which in its original version was not confined by moral hypocrisy or pent-up sexuality. Koko Head, for example, was originally called Kohelepelepe ("vagina labia minor") in reference to the time when Pele was attacked by Kamapua'a. To save Pele from being raped by the pig demigod, her older sister Kapo detached her vagina, using it as a decoy to divert Kamapua'a, and then hurled it to O'ahu, where it landed at the current site called Koko Head Crater. The missionary cartographers must have been tortured for several days before finally renaming the crater Koko Head!

Recently there has been an effort to translate Hawaiian tales collected in the nineteenth century into English without imposing the moral sensibilities felt by the earlier *haole* writers. For example, *Stories and Legends of Oahu* by Samuel M. Kamakau is a translation of nineteenth-century tales which includes several "trickster" stories that are reflective of the more lively and hilarious earthiness of the old Hawaiian storytellers. In one tale, a group of brothers are on a hike in Nuʻuanu Valley when the youngest *kolohe* (rascal) brother runs ahead. Later, his older siblings come across a *kukui* tree covered with rich sap. Sampling the gooey substance which the Hawaiians used as a gum, they all note that the sap is terribly rancid and spit it out in disgust. When they hear laughter from the top of the tree, they discover to their dismay that the sap is, in fact, the *kukai* (excrement) of their *kolohe* brother, who has been defecating in the tree! The quick censorship which this tale would have engendered by its *haole* editors and translators is not difficult to imagine. Fortunately, for the modern folklorist, storyteller and reader, the original Hawaiian versions were published in native newspapers and are now becoming more and more accessible to the non-Hawaiian-language reader.

Whatever their editor's motives, biases or subtle distortions, the stories reprinted in this collection still perpetuate the beauty and mystery of Hawaiian sacred narratives. The stories serve as an excellent first introduction to the myths, legends and folk tales which once bonded human life, the islands and the spirit realm in a cosmic unity of purpose. For those without the benefit of a Papakala to weave history and lore into a tapestry of cultural visions, the written word is a necessary first beginning. Then, after reading this collection, try to take the next step by visiting the sites mentioned in the text. Sitting quietly in the vicinity of the beach, stone, mountain or valley described in these tales of gods and ghost-gods, see if you don't experience the transforming power of the sacred narratives which for centuries have excited the souls of Polynesians. If even a small glimpse of that vision is afforded to you, then never again will you be able to see the lands and seas of Hawai'i in quite the same light without recognizing the *mana* of an older sense of place which must be respected, perpetuated and wherever possible, restored.

INTRODUCTION

The legends of the Hawaiian Islands are as diverse as those of any country in the world. They are also entirely distinct in form and thought from the fairy-tales which excite the interest and wonder of the English and German children. The mythology of Hawaii follows the laws upon which all myths are constructed. The Islanders have developed some beautiful nature-myths. Certain phenomena have been observed and the imagination has fitted the story to the interesting object which has attracted attention.

Now the Rainbow Maiden of Manoa, a valley lying back of Honolulu, is the story of a princess whose continual death and resurrection were invented to harmonize with the formation of a series of exquisite rainbows which are born on the mountain-sides in the upper end of the valley and die when the mist clouds reach the plain into which the valley opens. Then there were the fish of the Hawaiian Islands which vie with the butterflies of South America in their multitudinous combinations of colors. These imaginative people wondered how the fish were painted, so for a story a battle between two chiefs was either invented or taken as a basis. The chiefs fought on the mountain-sides until finally one was driven into the sea and compelled to make the deep waters his continual abiding-place. Here he found a unique and pleasant occupation in calling the various kinds of fish to his submarine home and then painting them in gay hues according to the dictates of his fancy. Thus we have a pure nature-myth developed from the love of the beautiful, one of the highest emotions dwelling in the hearts of the Hawaiians of the long ago.

So, again, Maui, a wonder-working hero like the Hercules of Grecian mythology, heard the birds sing, and noted their beautiful forms as they flitted from tree to tree and mingled their bright plumage with the leaves of the fragrant blossoms.

No other one of those who lived in the long ago could see what Maui saw. They heard the mysterious music, but the songsters were invisible. Many were the fancies concerning these strange creatures whom they could hear but could not see. Maui finally pitied his friends and made the birds visible. Ever since, man has been able to both hear the music and see the beauty of his forest neighbors.

Such nature-myths as these are well worthy of preservation by the side of any European fairy-tale. In purity of thought, vividness of imagination, and delicacy of coloring the Hawaiian myths are to be given a high place in literature among the stories of nature vivified by the imagination.

Another side of Hawaiian folk-lore is just as worthy of comparison. Lovers of "Jack-the-Giant-Killer," and of the many wonder-workers dwelling in the mist-lands of other nations, would enjoy reading the marvelous record of Maui, the skilful demi-god of Hawaii, who went fishing with a magic hook, and pulled up from the depths of the ocean groups of islands. This story is told in a matter-of-fact way, as if it were a fishing-excursion only a little out of the ordinary course. Maui lived in a land where volcanic fires were always burning in the mountains. Nevertheless it was a little inconvenient to walk thirty or forty miles for a live coal after the chill winds of the night had put out the fire which had been carefully protected the day before. Thus, when he saw that some intelligent birds knew the art of making a fire, he captured the leader and forced him to tell the secret of rubbing certain sticks together until fire came.

Maui also made snares, captured the sun and compelled it to journey regularly and slowly across the heavens. Thus the day was regulated to meet the wants of mankind. He lifted the heavens after they had rested so long upon all the plants that their leaves were flat.

There was a ledge of rock in one of the rivers, so Maui uprooted a tree and pushed it through, making an easy passage for both water and man. He invented many helpful articles for the use of mankind, but meanwhile frequently filled the days of his friends with trouble on account of the mischievous pranks which he played on them.

Fairies and gnomes dwelt in the woodland, coming forth at night to build temples, or massive walls, to fashion canoes, or whisper warnings. The birds and the fishes were capable and intelligent guardians over the households which had adopted them as protecting deities. Birds of brilliant plumage and sweet song were always faithful attendants on the chiefs, and able to converse with those over whom they kept watch. Sharks and other mighty fish of the deep waters were reliable messengers for those who rendered them sacrifices, often carrying their devotees from island to island and protecting them from many dangers.

Sometimes the gruesome and horrible creeps into Hawaiian folk-lore. A poison tree figures in the legends and finally becomes one of the most feared of all the gods of Hawaii. A cannibal dog, cannibal ghosts, and even a cannibal chief are prominent among the noted characters of the past.

Then the power of praying a person to death * with the aid of departed spirits was used, and is believed in, at the present time.

Almost every valley of the island has its peculiar and interesting myth. Often there is a historical foundation which has been dealt with fancifully and enlarged into miraculous proportions. There are hidden caves, which can be entered only by diving under the great breakers or into the deep waters of inland pools, around which cluster tales of love and adventure.

There are many mythological characters whose journeys extend to all the islands of the group. The Maui stories are not limited to the large island Hawaii and a part of the adjoining island which bears the name of Maui, but these stories are told in a garbled form on all the islands. So Pele, the fire-goddess, who dwelt in the hottest regions of the most active volcanoes, belongs to all, and also Kamapuaa, who is sometimes her husband, but more frequently her enemy. The conflicts between the two are often suggested by destructive lava flows checked by storms or ocean waves. It cannot be suspected that the ancient Hawaiian had the least idea of deifying fire and water—and yet the continual conflict

* Pule anaana.

between man and woman is like the eternal enmity between the two antagonistic elements of nature.

When the borders of mist-land are crossed, a rich store of folk-lore with a historical foundation is discovered. Chiefs and gods mingle together as in the days of the Nibelungen Lied. Voyages are made to many distant islands of the Pacific Ocean, whose names are frequently mentioned in the songs and tales of the wandering heroes. A chief from Samoa establishes a royal family on the largest of the Hawaiian Islands, and a chief from the Hawaiian group becomes a ruler in Tahiti.

Indeed the rovers of the Pacific have tales of seafaring which equal the accounts of the voyages of the Vikings.

The legends of the Hawaiian Islands are valuable in themselves, in that they reveal an understanding of the phenomena of nature and unveil their early history with its mythological setting. They are also valuable for comparison with the legends of the other Pacific islands, and they are exceedingly interesting when contrasted with the folk-lore of other nations.

The following legends treat of the worship of the lesser gods of Hawaii and of the domestic life of the Kanakas.

THE AUTHOR.

PRONUNCIATION

"A syllable in Hawaiian may consist of a single vowel, or a consonant united with a vowel or at most of a consonant and two vowels, never of more than one consonant. The accent of five-sixths of the words is on the penult, and a few proper names accent the first syllable.

In Hawaiian every syllable ends in a vowel and no syllable can have more than three letters, generally not more than two and a large number of syllables consist of single letters—vowels. Hence the vowel sounds greatly predominate over the consonant. The language may therefore appear monotonous to one unacquainted with its force.

In Hawaiian there is a great lack of generic terms, as is the case with all uncultivated languages. No people have use for generic terms until they begin to reason and the language shows that they were better warriors and poets than philosophers and statesmen. Their language, however, richly abounds in specific names and epithets.

The general rule, then, is that the accent falls on the penult; but there are many exceptions and some words which look the same to the eye take on entirely different meanings by different tones, accents, or inflections.

The study of these kaaos or legends would demonstrate that the Hawaiians possessed a language not only adapted to their former necessities but capable of being used in introducing the arts of civilized society and especially of pure morals, of law, and the religion of the Bible.''

The above quotations are from Lorrin Andrew's Dictionary of the Hawaiian Language, containing some 15,500 Hawaiian words, printed in Honolulu in 1865.

Hawaiian vowels
{
a is sounded as in father
e " " " " they
i " " " " marine
o " " " " note
u " " " " rule or as *oo* in moon
ai when sounded as a diphthong resembles English *ay*
au when sounded as a diphthong resembles *ou* as in loud
}

The consonants are *h, k, l, m, n, p,* and *w.* No distinction is made between *k* and *t* or *l* and *r,* and *w* sounds like *v* between the penult and final syllable of a word.

PART I

LEGENDS

I

THE GHOST OF WAHAULA TEMPLE

HAWAIIAN temples were never works of art. Broken lava was always near the site. Unhewn stones were piled into massive walls and laid in terraces for altar and floors. Water-worn pebbles were carried from the beach and strewn over the floor, making a smooth place for the naked feet of the temple dwellers to pass without injury from the sharp-edged lava. Rude grass huts built on terraces were the abodes of the priests and high chiefs who visited the places of sacrifice. Elevated, flat-topped piles of stones were built at one end of the temple for the chief idols and the sacrifices placed before them. Simplicity of detail marked every step of temple erection.

No hewn pillars or arched gateways of even the most primitive designs can be found in any of the temples whether of recent date or belonging to remote antiquity. There was no attempt at ornamentation even in the images of the great gods which they worshipped. Crude and hideous were the images before which they offered sacrifice and prayer. In themselves the heiaus, or temples, of the Hawaiian Islands have but little attraction. To-day they seem more like massive walled cattle-pens than places which have been used for worship. On the southeast coast of Hawaii near Kalapana is one of the largest, oldest, and best preserved heiaus. It is worthy the name of temple only as it is intimately associated with the religious customs of the Hawaiians. Its walls are several feet thick and in places ten to twelve feet high. It is divided into rooms or pens, in one of which still lies the huge sacrificial stone upon which victims —sometimes human—were slain before the bodies were placed as offerings in front of the hideous idols leaning against the stone walls.

This heiau is now called Wahaula (red-mouth). In ancient times it was known as Ahaula (the red assembly), possibly denoting that at times the priests and their attendants wore red mantles in their processions or during some part of their sacred ceremonies.

This temple is said to be the oldest of all the Hawaiian heiaus—except possibly the heiau at Kohala on the northern coast of the same island. These two heiaus date back in tradition to the time of Paao, the priest from Upolu, Samoa, who was said to have built them. He was the traditional father of the priestly line which ran parallel to the royal genealogy of the Kamehamehas during several centuries until the last high priest, Hewahewa, became a follower of Jesus Christ— the Saviour of the world. This was the last heiau destroyed when the ancient tabus and ceremonial rites were overthrown by the chiefs just before the coming of Christian missionaries. At that time the grass houses of the priests were burned and in these raging flames were thrown the wooden idols back of the altars and the bamboo huts of the soothsayers and the rude images on the walls, with everything combustible which belonged to the ancient order of worship. Only the walls and rough stone floors were left in the temple.

In the outer temple court was the most noted sacred grave in all the islands. Earth had been carried from the mountain-sides inland. Leaves and decaying trees added to the permanency of the soil. Here in a most unlikely place it was said that all the varieties of trees then found in the islands had been gathered by the priests—

the descendants of Paao. To this day the grave stands by the temple walls, an object of superstitious awe among the natives. Many of the varieties of trees planted there have died, leaving only those which were more hardy and needed less priestly care than they received a hundred years or more ago.

The temple is built near the coast on the rough, sharp, broken rocks of an ancient lava flow. In many places in and around the temple the lava was dug out, making holes three or four feet across and from one to two feet deep. These in the days of the priesthood had been filled with earth brought in baskets from the mountains. Here they raised sweet potatoes and taro and bananas. Now the rains have washed the soil away and to the unknowing there is no sign of previous agriculture. Near these depressions and along the paths leading to Wahaula other holes were sometimes cut out of the hard fine-grained lava. When heavy rains fell, little grooves carried the drops of water to these holes and they became small cisterns. Here the thirsty messengers running from one priestly clan to another, or the traveller or worshippers coming to the sacred place, could almost always find a few drops of water to quench their thirst.

Usually these water-holes were covered with a large flat stone under which the water ran into the cistern. To this day these small water-places border the path across the pahoehoe * lava field which lies adjacent to the broken a-a † lava upon which the Wahaula heiau is built. Many of them are still covered as in the days of the long ago.

It is not strange that legends have developed through the mists of the centuries around this rude old temple.

Wahaula was a tabu temple of the very highest rank. The native chants said,

"No keia heiau oia ke kapu enaena."

("Concerning this heiau is the burning tabu.")

"Enaena" means "burning with a red hot rage." The heiau was so thoroughly "tabu," or "kapu," that the smoke of its fires falling upon any of the people or even upon any one of the chiefs was sufficient cause for punishment by death, with the body as a sacrifice to the gods of the temple.

These gods were of the very highest rank among the Hawaiian deities. Certain days were tabu to Lono—or Rongo, as he was known in other island groups of the Pacific Ocean. Other days belonged to Ku—who was also worshipped from New Zealand to Tahiti. At other times Kane, known as Tane by many Polynesians, was held supreme. Then again Kanaloa—or

* Pahoehoe is smooth lava.   † A-a is rough lava.

Tanaroa, sometimes worshipped in Samoa and other island groups as the greatest of all their gods—had his days especially set apart for sacrifice and chant.

The Mu, or "body-catcher," of this heiau with his assistants seems to have been continually on the watch for human victims, and woe to the unfortunate man who carelessly or ignorantly walked where the winds blew the smoke from the temple fires. No one dared rescue him from the hands of the hunter of men—for then the wrath of all the gods was sure to follow him all the days of his life.

The people of the districts around Wahaula always watched the course of the winds with great anxiety, carefully noting the direction taken by the smoke. This smoke was the shadow cast by the deity worshipped, and was far more sacred than the shadow of the highest chief or king in all the islands.

It was always sufficient cause for death if a common man allowed his shadow to fall upon any tabu chief, i.e., a chief of especially high rank; but in this "burning tabu," if any man permitted the smoke or shadow of the god who was being worshipped in this temple to come near to him or overshadow him, it was a mark of such great disrespect that the god was supposed to be enaena, or red hot with rage.

Many ages ago a young chief whom we shall know by the name Kahele determined to take an especial journey around the island visiting all the noted and sacred places and becoming acquainted with the alii, or chiefs, of the other districts.

He passed from place to place, taking part with the chiefs who entertained him sometimes in the use of the papa-hee, or surf-board, riding the white-capped surf as it majestically swept shoreward—sometimes spending night after night in the innumerable gambling contests which passed under the name pili waiwai—and sometimes riding the narrow sled, or holua, with which Hawaiian chiefs raced down the steep grassed lanes. Then again, with a deep sense of the solemnity of sacred things, he visited the most noted of the heiaus and made contributions to the offerings before the gods. Thus the days passed, and the slow journey was very pleasant to Kahele.

In time he came to Puna, the district in which was located the temple Wahaula.

But alas! in the midst of the many stories of the past which he had heard, and the many pleasures he had enjoyed while on his journey, Kahele forgot the peculiar power of the tabu of the smoke of Wahaula. The fierce winds of the south were blowing and changing from

point to point. The young man saw the sacred
grove in the edge of which the temple walls
could be discerned. Thin wreaths of smoke were
tossed here and there from the temple fires.

Kahele hastened toward the temple. The Mu
was watching his coming and joyfully marking
him as a victim. The altars of the gods were
desolate, and if but a particle of smoke fell upon
the young man no one could keep him from
the hands of the executioner.

The perilous moment came. The warm
breath of one of the fires touched the young
chief's cheek. Soon a blow from the club of
the Mu laid him senseless on the rough stones
of the outer court of the temple. The smoke of
the wrath of the gods had fallen upon him, and
it was well that he should lie as a sacrifice upon
their altars.

Soon the body with the life still in it was
thrown across the sacrificial stone. Sharp
knives made from the strong wood of the bamboo
let his life-blood flow down the depressions across
the face of the stone. Quickly the body was
dismembered and offered as a sacrifice.

For some reason the priests, after the flesh
had decayed, set apart the bones for some
special purpose. The legends imply that the
bones were to be treated dishonorably. It may
have been that the bones were folded together

and known as unihipili, bones, folded and laid
away for purposes of incantation. Such bundles
of bones were put through a process of prayers
and charms until at last it was thought a new
spirit was created which dwelt in that bundle
and gave the possessor a peculiar power in deeds
of witchcraft.

The spirit of Kahele rebelled against this disposition of all that remained of his body. He
wanted to be back in his native district, that
he might enjoy the pleasures of the Under-world
with his own chosen companions. Restlessly
the spirit haunted the dark corners of the temple,
watching the priests as they handled his bones.

Helplessly the ghost fumed and fretted against
its condition. It did all that a disembodied spirit
could do to attract the attention of the priests.

At last the spirit fled by night from this place
of torment to the home which he had so joyfully
left a short time before.

Kahele's father was the high chief of Kau.
Surrounded by retainers, he passed his days in
quietness and peace waiting for the return of
his son.

One night a strange dream came to him. He
heard a voice calling from the mysterious con-
fines of the spirit-land. As he listened, a spirit
form stood by his side. The ghost was that of
his son Kahele.

By means of the dream the ghost revealed to the father that he had been put to death and that his bones were in great danger of dishonorable treatment.

The father awoke benumbed with fear, realizing that his son was calling upon him for immediate help. At once he left his people and journeyed from place to place secretly, not knowing where or when Kahele had died, but fully sure that the spirit of his vision was that of his son. It was not difficult to trace the young man. He had left his footprints openly all along the way. There was nothing of shame or dishonor—and the father's heart filled with pride as he hastened on.

From time to time, however, he heard the spirit voice calling him to save the bones of the body of his dead son. At last he felt that his journey was nearly done. He had followed the footsteps of Kahele almost entirely around the island, and had come to Puna—the last district before his own land of Kau would welcome his return.

The spirit voice could be heard now in the dream which nightly came to him. Warnings and directions were frequently given.

Then the chief came to the lava fields of Wahaula and lay down to rest. The ghost came to him again in a dream, telling him that great personal danger was near at hand. The chief was a very strong man, excelling in athletic and brave deeds, but in obedience to the spirit voice he rose early in the morning, secured oily nuts from a kukui*-tree, beat out the oil, and anointed himself thoroughly.

Walking along carelessly as if to avoid suspicion, he drew near to the lands of the temple Wahaula. Soon a man came out to meet him. This man was an Olohe, a beardless man belonging to a lawless robber clan which infested the district, possibly assisting the man-hunters of the temple in securing victims for the temple altars. This Olohe was very strong and self-confident, and thought he would have but little difficulty in destroying this stranger who journeyed alone through Puna.

Almost all day the battle raged between the two men. Back and forth they forced each other over the lava beds. The chief's well-oiled body was very difficult for the Olohe to grasp. Bruised and bleeding from repeated falls on the rough lava, both of the combatants were becoming very weary. Then the chief made a new attack, forcing the Olohe into a narrow place from which there was no escape, and at last seizing him, breaking his bones, and then killing him.

As the shadows of night rested over the temple

---

* Aleurites Moluccana.

and its sacred grave the chief crept closer to
the dreaded tabu walls. Concealing himself
he waited for the ghost to reveal to him the best
plan for action. The ghost came, but was compelled to bid the father wait patiently for a fit
time when the secret place in which the bones
were hidden could be safely visited.

For several days and nights the chief hid himself near the temple. He secretly uttered the
prayers and incantations needed to secure the
protection of his family gods.

One night the darkness was very great, and the
priests and watchmen of the temple felt sure that
no one would attempt to enter the sacred precincts.
Deep sleep rested upon all the temple-dwellers.

Then the ghost of Kahele hastened to the place
where the father was sleeping and aroused him
for the dangerous task before him.

As the father arose he saw this ghost outlined
in the darkness, beckoning him to follow. Step
by step he felt his way cautiously over the rough
path and along the temple walls until he saw
the ghost standing near a great rock pointing at
a part of the wall.

The father seized a stone which seemed to
be the one most directly in the line of the ghost's
pointing. To his surprise it was removed very
easily from the wall. Back of it was a hollow
place in which lay a bundle of folded bones.

The ghost urged the chief to take these bones and depart quickly.

The father obeyed, and followed the spirit guide until safely away from the temple of the burning wrath of the gods. He carried the bones to Kau and placed them in his own secret family burial cave.

The ghost of Wahaula went down to the spirit world in great joy. Death had come. The life of the young chief had been taken for temple service and yet there had at last been nothing dishonorable connected with the destruction of the body and the passing away of the spirit.

GOURD BOTTLE

II

MALUAE AND THE UNDER–WORLD

THIS is a story from Manoa Valley, back of Honolulu. In the upper end of the valley, at the foot of the highest mountains on the island Oahu, lived Maluae. He was a farmer, and had chosen this land because rain fell abundantly on the mountains, and the streams brought down fine soil from the decaying forests and disintegrating rocks, fertilizing his plants.

Here he cultivated bananas* and taro † and sweet potatoes. His bananas grew rapidly by the sides of the brooks, and yielded large bunches of fruit from their tree-like stems; his taro filled small walled-in pools, growing in the water like water-lilies, until the roots were matured, when the plants were pulled up and the roots boiled and prepared for food; his sweet potatoes—a vegetable known among the ancient New Zealanders as ku-maru, and supposed to have come from Hawaii—were planted on the drier uplands.

Thus he had plenty of food continually growing, and ripening from time to time. Whenever he gathered any of his food products he brought a part to his family temple and placed it on an

* Maia or Musa sapientum.
† Calocasia antiquorum.

altar before the gods Kane and Kanaloa, then he took the rest to his home for his family to eat.

He had a boy whom he dearly loved, whose name was Kaa-lii (rolling chief). This boy was a careless, rollicking child.

One day the boy was tired and hungry. He passed by the temple of the gods and saw bananas, ripe and sweet, on the little platform before the gods. He took these bananas and ate them all.

The gods looked down on the altar expecting to find food, but it was all gone and there was nothing for them. They were very angry, and ran out after the boy. They caught him eating the bananas, and killed him. The body they left lying under the trees, and taking out his ghost threw it into the Under-world.

The father toiled hour after hour cultivating his food plants, and when wearied returned to his home. On the way he met the two gods. They told him how his boy had robbed them of their sacrifices and how they had punished him. They said, "We have sent his ghost body to the lowest regions of the Under-world."

The father was very sorrowful and heavy-hearted as he went on his way to his desolate home. He searched for the body of his boy, and at last found it. He saw too that the story of the gods was true, for partly eaten bananas filled the mouth, which was set in death.

He wrapped the body very carefully in kapa
cloth made from the bark of trees.* He
carried it into his rest-house and laid it on the
sleeping-mat. After a time he lay down beside
the body, refusing all food, and planning to die
with his boy. He thought if he could escape
from his own body he would be able to go down
where the ghost of his boy had been sent. If
he could find that ghost he hoped to take it to
the other part of the Under-world, where they
could be happy together.

He placed no offerings on the altar of the
gods. No prayers were chanted. The afternoon and evening passed slowly. The gods
waited for their worshipper, but he came not.
They looked down on the altar of sacrifice, but
there was nothing for them.

The night passed and the following day. The
father lay by the side of his son, neither eating
nor drinking, and longing only for death. The
house was tightly closed.

Then the gods talked together, and Kane said:
"Maluae eats no food, he prepares no awa to
drink, and there is no water by him. He is near
the door of the Under-world. If he should die,
we would be to blame."

Kanaloa said: "He has been a good man, but
now we do not hear any prayers. We are losing

* Trees used for kapa were the hau, olona, akala, maaloa, mamaki,
pouli, and wauke.

our worshipper. We in quick anger killed his son. Was this the right reward? He has called us morning and evening in his worship. He has provided fish and fruits and vegetables for our altars. He has always prepared awa* from the juice of the yellow awa root for us to drink. We have not paid him well for his care."

Then they decided to go and give life to the father, and permit him to take his ghost body and go down into Po, the dark land, to bring back the ghost of the boy. So they went to Maluae and told him they were sorry for what they had done.

The father was very weak from hunger, and longing for death, and could scarcely listen to them.

When Kane said, "Have you love for your child?" the father whispered: "Yes. My love is without end." "Can you go down into the dark land and get that spirit and put it back in the body which lies here?"

"No," the father said, "no, I can only die and go to live with him and make him happier by taking him to a better place."

Then the gods said, "We will give you the power to go after your boy and we will help you to escape the dangers of the land of ghosts."

Then the father, stirred by hope, rose up and took food and drink. Soon he was strong enough to go on his journey.

* Piper methysticum.

The gods gave him a ghost body and also prepared a hollow stick like bamboo, in which they put food, battle-weapons, and a piece of burning lava for fire.

Not far from Honolulu is a beautiful modern estate with fine roads, lakes, running brooks, and interesting valleys extending back into the mountain range. This is called by the very ancient name Moanalua (two lakes). Near the seacoast of this estate was one of the most noted ghost localities of the islands. The ghosts after wandering over the island Oahu would come to this place to find a way into their real home, the Under-world or Po.

Here was a ghostly breadfruit-tree* named Lei-walo, possibly meaning "the eight wreaths" or "the eighth wreath"—the last wreath of leaves from the land of the living which would meet the eyes of the dying.

The ghosts would leap or fly or climb into the branches of this tree, trying to find a rotten branch upon which they could sit until it broke and threw them into the dark sea below.

Maluae climbed up the breadfruit-tree. He found a branch where ghosts were sitting waiting for it to fall. His weight was so much greater than theirs that the branch broke at once, and down they all fell into the land of Po.

He needed merely to taste the food in his hollow

* Ulu or Artocarpus incisa.

cane to have new life and strength. This he had
done when he climbed the tree; thus he had been
able to push past the fabled guardians of the
pathway of the ghosts in the Upper-world. As
he entered the Under-world he again tasted the
food of the gods and he felt himself growing
stronger and stronger.

He took a magic war-club and a spear out of
the cane given by the gods. Ghostly warriors
tried to hinder his entrance into the different
districts of the dark land. The spirits of dead
chiefs challenged him when he passed their
homes. Battle after battle was fought. His
magic club struck the warriors down, and his
spear tossed them aside.

Sometimes he was warmly greeted and aided
by ghosts of kindly spirit. Thus he went from
place to place, searching for his boy, finding him
at last, as the Hawaiians quaintly expressed it,
"down in the papa-ku" (the established foundation of Po), choking and suffocating from the
bananas of ghost-land which he was compelled
to continually force into his mouth.

The father caught the spirit of the boy and
started back toward the Upper-world, but the
ghosts surrounded him. They tried to catch
him and take the spirit away from him. Again
the father partook of the food of the gods. Once
more he wielded his war-club, but the hosts of

enemies were too great. Multitudes arose on all sides, crushing him by their overwhelming numbers.

At last he raised his magic hollow cane and took the last portion of food. Then he poured out the portion of burning lava which the gods had placed inside. It fell upon the dry floor of the Under-world. The flames dashed into the trees and the shrubs of ghost-land. Fire-holes opened and streams of lava burst out.

Backward fled the multitudes of spirits. The father thrust the spirit of the boy quickly into the empty magic cane and rushed swiftly up to his home-land. He brought the spirit to the body lying in the rest-house and forced it to find again its living home.

Afterward the father and the boy took food to the altars of the gods, and chanted the accustomed prayers heartily and loyally all the rest of their lives.

GOURD DRUM

III

A GIANT'S ROCK–THROWING

A POINT of land on the northwestern coast of the island Oahu is called Ka-lae-o-Kaena which means "The Cape of Kaena."

A short distance from this cape lies a large rock which bears the name Pohaku-o-Kauai, or rock of Kauai, a large island northwest of Oahu. This rock is as large as a small house.

There is an interesting legend told on the island of Oahu which explains why these names have for generations been fastened to the cape and to the rock. A long time ago there lived on Kauai a man of wonderful power, Hau-pu. When he was born, the signs of a demi-god were over the house of his birth. Lightning flashed through the skies, and thunder reverberated—a rare event in the Hawaiian Islands, and supposed to be connected with the birth or death or some very unusual occurrence in the life of a chief.

Mighty floods of rain fell and poured in torrents down the mountain-sides, carrying the red iron soil into the valleys in such quantities that the rapids and the waterfalls became the color of blood, and the natives called this a blood-rain.

During the storm, and even after sunshine filled the valley, a beautiful rainbow rested over the house in which the young chief was born. This rainbow was thought to come from the miraculous powers of the new-born child shining out from him instead of from the sunlight around him. Many chiefs throughout the centuries of Hawaiian legends were said to have had this rainbow around them all their lives.

Hau-pu while a child was very powerful, and after he grew up was widely known as a great warrior. He would attack and defeat armies of his enemies without aid from any person. His spear was like a mighty weapon, sometimes piercing a host of enemies, and sometimes putting aside all opposition when he thrust it into the ranks of his opponents.

If he had thrown his spear and if fighting with his bare hands did not vanquish his foes, he would leap to the hillside, tear up a great tree, and with it sweep away all before him as if he were wielding a huge broom. He was known and feared throughout all the Hawaiian Islands. He became angry quickly and used his great powers very rashly.

One night he lay sleeping in his royal rest-house on the side of a mountain which faced the neighboring island of Oahu. Between the two islands lay a broad channel about thirty miles wide. When clouds were on the face of the sea, these islands were hidden from each other; but when they lifted, the rugged valleys of the mountains on one island could be clearly seen from the other. Even by moonlight the shadowy lines would appear.

This night the strong man stirred in his sleep. Indistinct noises seemed to surround his house. He turned over and dropped off into slumber again.

Soon he was aroused a second time, and he was awake enough to hear shouts of men far, far away. Louder rose the noise mixed with the roar of the great surf waves, so he realized that it came from the sea, and he then forced himself to rise and stumble to the door.

He looked out toward Oahu. A multitude of lights were flashing on the sea before his sleepy eyes. A low murmur of many voices came from the place where the dancing lights seemed to be. His confused thoughts made it appear to him that a great fleet of warriors was coming from Oahu to attack his people.

He blindly rushed out to the edge of a high precipice which overlooked the channel. Evidently many boats and many people were out in the sea below.

He laughed, and stooped down and tore a huge rock from its place. This he swung back and forth, back and forth, back and forth, until he gave it great impetus which added to his own miraculous power sent it far out over the sea. Like a great cloud it rose in the heavens and, as if blown by swift winds, sped on its way.

Over on the shores of Oahu a chief whose name was Kaena had called his people out for a night's fishing. Canoes large and small came from all along the coast. Torches without number had been made and placed in the canoes. The largest fish-nets had been brought.

There was no need of silence. Nets had been set in the best places. Fish of all kinds were to be aroused and frightened into the nets. Flashing lights, splashing paddles, and clamor from hundreds of voices resounded all around the nets.

Gradually the canoes came nearer and nearer the centre. The shouting increased. Great joy ruled the tumult which drowned the roar of the waves.

Across the channel and up the mountain-sides of Kauai swept the shouts of the fishing-party. Into the ears of drowsy Hau-pu the noise forced itself. Little dreamed the excited fishermen of the effect of this on far-away Kauai.

Suddenly something like a bird as large as a mountain seemed to be above, and then with a mighty sound like the roar of winds it descended upon them.

Smashed and submerged were the canoes when the huge boulder thrown by Hau-pu hurled itself upon them.

The chief Kaena and his canoe were in the centre of this terrible mass of wreckage, and he and many of his people lost their lives.

The waves swept sand upon the shore until in time a long point of land was formed. The remaining followers of the dead chief named this cape "Kaena."

The rock thrown by Hau-pu embedded itself in the depths of the ocean, but its head rose far above the water, even when raging storms dashed turbulent waves against it. To this death-dealing rock the natives gave the name "Rock of Kauai."

Thus for generations has the deed of the man of giant force been remembered on Oahu, and so have a cape and a rock received their names.

IV

KALO–EKE–EKE, THE TIMID TARO

A MYTH is a purely imaginative story. A legend is a story with some foundation in fact. A fable tacks on a moral. A tradition is a myth or legend or fact handed down from generation to generation.

The old Hawaiians were frequently myth-makers. They imagined many a fairy-story for the different localities of the islands, and these are very interesting. The myth of the two taro plants belongs to South Kona, Hawaii, and affords an excellent illustration of Hawaiian imagination. The story is told in different ways, and came to the writer in the present form:

A chief lived on the mountain-side above Hookena. There his people cultivated taro, made kapa cloth, and prepared the trunks of koa-trees for canoes. He had a very fine taro patch. The plants prided themselves upon their rapid and perfect growth.

In one part of the taro pond, side by side, grew two taro plants—finer, stronger, and more beautiful than the others. The leaf stalks bent over in more perfect curves: the leaves developed in graceful proportions. Mutual admiration

filled the hearts of the two taro* plants and re-
sulted in pledges of undying affection.

One day the chief was talking to his servants
about the food to be made ready for a feast. He
ordered the two especially fine taro plants to be
pulled up. One of the servants came to the
home of the two lovers and told them that they
were to be taken by the chief.

Because of their great affection for each other
they determined to cling to life as long as possible,
and therefore moved to another part of the taro
patch, leaving their neighbors to be pulled up
instead of themselves.

But the chief soon saw them in their new home
and again ordered their destruction. Again they
fled. This happened from time to time until
the angry chief determined that they should be
taken, no matter what part of the pond they
might be in.

The two taro plants thought best to flee,
therefore took to themselves wings and made a
short flight to a neighboring taro patch. Here
again their enemy found them. A second flight
was made to another part of South Kona, and
then to still another, until all Kona was interested in the perpetual pursuit and the perpetual
escape. At last there was no part of Kona in
which they could be concealed. A friend of the
angry chief would reveal their hiding-place, while

* Also kalo, Calocasia antiquorum.

one of their own friends would give warning of the coming of their pursuer. At last they leaped into the air and flew on and on until they were utterly weary and fell into a taro patch near Waiohinu. But their chief had ordered the imu (cooking-place) to be made ready for them, and had hastened along the way on foot, trying to capture them if at any time they should try to alight. However, their wings moved more swiftly than his feet, so they had a little rest before he came near to their new home. Then again they lifted themselves into the sky. Favoring winds carried them along and they flew a great distance away from South Kona into the neighboring district of Kau. Here they found a new home under a kindly chief. Here they settled down and lived many years under the name of Kalo-eke-eke, or "The Timid Taro." A large family grew up about them and a happy old age blessed their declining days.

It is possible that this beautiful little story may have grown out of the ancient Hawaiian unwritten law which sometimes permitted the subjects of a chief to move away from their home and transfer their allegiance to some neighboring ruler.

V

LEGENDARY CANOE-MAKING

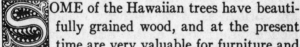OME of the Hawaiian trees have beauti-
fully grained wood, and at the present
time are very valuable for furniture and
interior decoration. The koa* is probably the
best of the trees of this class. It is known as
the Hawaiian mahogany. The grain is very fine
and curly and wavy, and is capable of a very high
polish. The koa still grows luxuriantly on the
steep sides and along the ridges of the high mountains of all the islands of the Hawaiian group. It
has great powers of endurance. It is not easily
worn by the pebbles and sand of the beach, nor
is it readily split or broken by the tempestuous
waves of the ocean, therefore from time immemo-
rial the koa has been the tree for the canoe and
surf-board of the Hawaiians. Long and large
have been the canoes hewn from the massive
tree trunks by the aid of the koi-pohaku, the
cutting stone, or adze, of ancient Hawaii. Sometimes these canoes were given miraculous powers
of motion so that they swept through the seas
more rapidly than the swiftest shark. Often
the god of the winds, who had special care

* Acacia koa.

over some one of the high chiefs, would carry him
from island to island in a canoe which never
rested when calms prevailed or stopped when
fierce waves wrenched, but bore the chief swiftly
and unfailingly to the desired haven.

There is a delightful little story about a chief
who visited the most northerly island, Kauai.
He found the natives of that island feasting and
revelling in all the abandon of savage life. Sports
and games innumerable were enjoyed. Thus
day and night passed until, as the morning of a
new day dawned, an unwonted stir along the
beach made manifest some event of very great
importance. The new chief apparently cared
but little for all the excitement. The king of
the island had sent one of his royal ornaments
to a small island some miles distant from the
Kauai shores. He was blessed with a daughter
so beautiful that all the available chiefs desired
her for wife. The father, hoping to avoid the
complications which threatened to involve his
household with the households of the jealous
suitors, announced that he would give his
daughter to the man who secured the ornament
from the far-away island. It was to be a canoe
race with a wife for the prize.

The young chiefs waited for the hour appointed.
Their well-polished koa canoes lined the beach.
The stranger chief made no preparation, Quietly

he enjoyed the gibes and taunts hurled from one to another by the young chiefs. Laughingly he requested permission to join in the contest, receiving as the reward for his request a look of approbation from the handsome chiefess.

The word was given. The well-manned canoes were pushed from the shore and forced out through the inrolling surf. In the rush some of the boats were interlocked with others, some filled with water, while others safely broke away from the rest and passed out of sight toward the coveted island. Still the stranger seemed to be in no haste to win the prize. The face of the chiefess grew dark with disappointment.

At last the stranger launched his finely polished canoe and called one of his followers to sail with him. It seemed to be utterly impossible for him to even dream of securing the prize, but the canoe began to move as if it had the wings of a swift bird or the fins of fleetest fish. He had taken for his companion in his magic canoe one of the gods controlling the ocean winds. He was first to reach the island. Then he came swiftly back for his bride. He made his home among his new friends.

The Hawaiians had many interesting ceremonies in connection with the process of securing the tree and fashioning it into a canoe.

David Malo, a Hawaiian writer of about the

year 1840, says, "The building of a canoe was a
religious matter." When a man found a fine koa-
tree he went to the priest whose province was
canoe-making and said, "I have found a koa-tree,
a fine large tree." On receiving this information
the priest went at night to sleep before his shrine.
If in his sleep he had a vision of some one
standing naked before him, he knew that the
koa-tree was rotten, and would not go up into
the woods to cut that tree. If another tree was
found and he dreamed of a handsome well-dressed
man or woman standing before him, when he
awoke he felt sure that the tree would make a
good canoe. Preparations were made accordingly
to go into the mountains and hew the koa into
a canoe. They took with them as offerings a
pig, coconuts, red fish, and awa. Having come
to the place they rested for the night, sacrificing
these things to the gods.

Sometimes, when a royal canoe was to be
prepared, it seems as if human beings were also
brought and slain at the root of the tree. There is
no record of cannibalism connected with these
sacrifices, and yet when the pig and fish had
been offered before the tree, usually a hole was
dug close to the tree and an oven prepared in
which the meat and vegetables were cooked for
the morning feast of the canoe-makers. The tree
was carefully examined and the signs and por-

tents noted. The song of a little bird would frequently cause an entire change in the enterprise.

When the time came to cut down the tree the priest would take his stone axe and offer prayer to the male and female deities who were supposed to be the special patrons of canoebuilding, showing them the axe, and saying: "Listen now to the axe. This is the axe which is to cut down the tree for the canoe."

David Malo says: "When the tree began to crack, ready to fall, they lowered their voices and allowed no one to make a disturbance. When the tree had fallen, the head priest mounted the trunk and called out, 'Smite with the axe, and hollow the canoe.' This was repeated again and again as he walked along the fallen tree, marking the full length of the desired canoe."

Dr. Emerson gives the following as one of the prayers sometimes used by the priest when passing along the trunk of the tree:

> "Grant a canoe which shall be swift as a fish
> To sail in stormy seas
> When the storm tosses on all sides."

After the canoe had been roughly shaped, the ends pointed, the bottom rounded, and perhaps a portion of the inside of the log removed, the people fastened lines to the canoe to haul it down to the beach. When they were ready for the work the priest again prayed: "Oh, canoe gods, look you after this canoe. Guard it from stem to stern, until it is placed in the canoe-house."

Then the canoe was hauled by the people in front, or held back by those who were in the rear, until it had passed all the hard and steep places along the mountain-side and been put in place for the finishing touches. When completed, pig and fish and fruits were again offered to the gods. Sometimes human beings were again a part of the sacrifice.

Prayers and incantations were part of the ceremony. There was to be no disturbance or noise, or else it would be dangerous for its owner to go out in his new canoe. If all the people except the priest had been quiet, the canoe was pronounced safe.

It is said that the ceremony of lashing the outrigger to the canoe was of very great solemnity, probably because the ability to pass through the high surf waves depended so much upon the outrigger as a balance which kept the canoe from being overturned.

The story of Laka and the fairies is told to illustrate the difficulties surrounding canoe-making. Laka desired to make a fine canoe, and sought through the forests for the best tree available. Taking his stone axe he toiled all day until the tree was felled. Then he went home to rest. On the morrow he could not find the log. The trees of the forest had been apparently undisturbed. Again he cut a tree, and once more could not find the log. At last he cut a tree and watched in the night. Then he saw in the night shadows a host of the little people who toil with miraculous powers to support them. They raised the tree and set it in its place and restored it to its wonted appearance among its fellows. But Laka caught the king of the gnomes and from him learned how to gain the aid rather than the opposition of the little people. By their help his canoe was taken to the shore and fashioned into beautiful shape for wonderful and successful voyages.

VI

LAU–KA–IEIE

"Waipio Valley, the beautiful:
Precipices around it,
The sea on one side;
The precipices are hard to climb;
Not to be climbed
Are the sea precipices."

—*Hawaiian Chant.*

KAKEA (the white one) and Kaholo (the runner) were the children of the Valley. Their parents were the precipices which were sheer to the sea, and could only be passed by boats. They married, and Kaholo conceived. The husband said, "If a boy is born, I will name it; if a girl, you give the name."

He went up to see his sister Pokahi, and asked her to go swiftly to see his wife. Pokahi's husband was Kaukini, a bird-catcher. He went out into the forest for some birds. Soon he came back and prepared them for cooking. Hot stones were put inside the birds and the birds were packed in calabashes, carefully covered over with wet leaves, which made steam inside so the birds were well cooked. Then they were brought to Kaholo for a feast.

On their way they went down to Waipio Valley,

coming to the foot of the precipice. Pokahi wanted some sea-moss and some shell-fish, so she told the two men to go on while she secured these things to take to Kaholo. She gathered the soft lipoa* moss and went up to the water-fall, to Ulu (Kaholo's home). The baby was born, wrapped in the moss and thrown into the sea, making a shapeless bundle, but a kupua (sorcerer) saw that a child was there. The child was taken and washed clean in the soft lipoa, and cared for. All around were the signs of the birth of a chief.

They named him Hiilawe, and from him the Waipio waterfall has its name, according to the saying, "Falling into mist is the water of Hii-lawe."

Pokahi took up her package in which she had brought the moss and shell-fish, but the moss was gone. Hina-ulu-ohia (Hina-the-growing-ohia-tree) was the sorcerer who took the child in the lipoa moss. She was the aumakua, or ancestor goddess, of the boat-builders.

Pokahi dreamed that a beautiful woman ap-peared, her body covered with the leaves of ohia †-trees. "I know that you have not had any child. I will now give you one. Awake, and go to the Waipio River; watch thirty days, then you will find a girl wrapped in soft moss. This

---

* Haliseris plagiogramma.   † Metrosideros rugosa.

shall be your adopted child. I will show you how to care for it. Your brother and his wife must not know. Your husband alone may know about this adopted girl."

Pokahi and her husband went down at once to the mouth of the river, heard an infant cry in the midst of red-colored mist, and found a child wrapped in the fragrant moss. She wished to take it up, but was held back by magic powers. She saw an ohia-tree rising up from the water, —branches, leaves, and flowers,—and iiwi (birds) coming to pick the flowers. The red birds and red flowers were very beautiful. This tree was Hina. The birds began to sing, and quietly the tree sank down into the water and disappeared, the birds flying away to the west.

Pokahi returned to her brother's house, going down to the sea every day, where she saw the human form of the child growing in the shelter of that red mist on the surface of the sea. At the end of the thirty days Pokahi told her friends and her husband that they must go back home. On their way they went to the river. She told her husband to look at the red mist, but he wanted to hurry on. As they approached their house, cooking-odors welcomed them, and they found plenty of food prepared outside. They saw something moving inside. The trees seemed to be walking as if with the feet of men. Steps were heard, and voices were calling for the people of the house.

Kaukini prepared a lamp, and Pokahi in a vision saw the same fine tree which she had seen before. There was also a *hala-tree with its beautiful yellow blossoms. As they looked they saw leaves of different kinds falling one after another, making in one place a soft fragrant bed.

Then a woman and a man came with an infant. They were the god Ku and Hina his wife. They said to Pokahi and her husband, "We have accepted your sacrifices and have seen that you are childless, so now we have brought you this child to adopt." Then they disappeared among the trees of the forest, leaving the child, Lau-ka-†ieie (leaf of the ieie vine). She was well cared for and grew up into a beautiful woman without fault or blemish. Her companions and servants were the birds and the flowers.

Lau-ka-pali (leaf of the precipice) was one of her friends. One day she made whistles of ti‡ leaves, and blew them. The Leaf-of-the-Morning-Glory saw that the young chiefess liked this, so she went out and found Pupu-kani-oi (the singing land-shell), whose home was on the leaves of the forest trees. Then she found another Pupu-hina-hina-ula (shell-beautiful with rainbow

---

* Hala, lahala, puhala,—Pandanus adoratissimus.
† Freycinetia Arnotti.
‡ Ki or lauki, Cordyline terminalis.

colors). In the night the shells sang, and their voices stole their way into the love of Lau-ka-ieie, so she gently sang with them.

Nohu-ua-palai (a fern), one of the old residents of that place, went out into the forest, and, hearing the voices of the girl and the shells, came to the house. She chanted her name, but there was no reply. All was silent. At last, Pua-ohelo (the blossom of the ohelo*), one of the flowers in the house, heard, and opening the door, invited her to come in and eat.

Nohu-ua-palai went in and feasted with the girls. Lau-ka-ieie dreamed about Kawelona (the setting of the sun), at Lihue, a fine young man, the first-born of one of the high chiefs of Kauai. She told her kahu (guardian) all about her dream and the distant island. The kahu asked who should go to find the man of the dream. All the girl friends wanted to go. She told them to raise their hands and the one who had the longest fingers could go. This was Pupu-kani-oi (the singing shell). The leaf family all sobbed as they bade farewell to the shell.

The shell said: "Oh, my leaf-sisters Laukoa [leaf of the koa-tree] and Lauanau [leaf of the paper-mulberry tree], arise, go with me on my journey! Oh, my shell-sisters of the blue sea, come to the beach, to the sand! Come and show me the path I am to go! Oh, Pupu-

* Vaccinium penduliformis.

moka-lau [the land-shell clinging to the moki-
hana* leaf], come and look at me, for I am one
of your family! Call all the shells to aid me
in my journey! Come to me!"

Then she summoned her brother, Makani-kau,
chief of the winds, to waft them away in their
wind bodies. They journeyed all around the
island of Hawaii to find some man who would
be like the man of the dream. They found no
one there nor on any of the other islands up to
Oahu, where the Singing Shell fell in love with
a chief and turned from her journey, but Makani-
kau went on to Kauai.

Ma-eli-eli, the dragon woman of Heeia, tried
to persuade him to stop, but on he went. She
ran after him. Limaloa, the dragon of Laiewai,
also tried to catch Makani-kau, but he was too
swift. On the way to Kauai, Makani-kau saw
some people in a boat chased by a big shark. He
leaped on the boat and told them he would play
with the shark and they could stay near but
need not fear. Then he jumped into the sea.
The shark turned over and opened its mouth
to seize him; he climbed on it, caught its fins,
and forced it to flee through the water. He
drove it to the shore and made it fast among
the rocks. It became the great shark stone,
Koa-mano (warrior shark), at Haena. He leaped
from the shark to land, the boat following.

* Pelea anisata.

He saw the hill of "Fire-Throwing," a place where burning sticks were thrown over the precipices, a very beautiful sight at night. He leaped to the top of the hill in his shadow body. Far up on the hill was a vast number of iiwi (birds). Makani-kau went to them as they were flying toward Lehua. They only felt the force of the winds, for they could not see him or his real body. He saw that the birds were carrying a fine man as he drew near.

This was the one Lau-ka-ieie desired for her husband. They carried this boy on their wings easily and gently over the hills and sea toward the sunset island, Lehua. There they slowly flew to earth. They were the bird guardians of Kawelona, and when they travelled from place to place they were under the direction of the bird-sorcerer, Kukala-a-ka-manu.

Kawelona had dreamed of a beautiful girl who had visited him again and again, so he was prepared to meet Makani-kau. He told his parents and adopted guardians and bird-priests about his dreams and the beautiful girl he wanted to marry.

Makani-kau met the winds of Niihau and Lehua, and at last was welcomed by the birds. He told Kawelona his mission, who prepared to go to Hawaii, asking how they should go. Makani-kau went to the seaside and called for his many bodies to come and give him the boat for the husband of their great sister Lau-ka-ieie. Thus he made known his mana, or spirit power, to Kawelona. He called on the great cloud-gods to send the long white cloud-boat, and it soon appeared. Kawelona entered the boat with fear, and in a few minutes lost sight of the island of Lehua and his bird guardians as he sailed out into the sea. Makani-kau dropped down by the side of a beautiful shell-boat, entered it, and stopped at Mana. There he took several girls and put them in a double canoe, or au-waa-olalua (spirit-boat).

Meanwhile the sorcerer ruler of the birds agreed to find out where Kawelona was to satisfy the longing of his parents, whom he had left without showing them where he was going or what dangers he might meet. The sorcerer poured water into a calabash and threw in two lehua flowers, which floated on the water. Then he turned his eyes toward the sun and prayed: "Oh, great sun, to whom belongs the heavens, turn your eyes downward to look on the water in this calabash, and show us what you see therein! Look upon the beautiful young woman. She is not one from Kauai. There is no one more beautiful than she. Her home is under the glowing East, and a royal rainbow is around her. There are beautiful girls attending her."

The sorcerer saw the sun-pictures in the water, and interpreted to the friends the journey of Kawelona, telling them it was a long, long way, and they must wait patiently many days for any word. In the signs he saw the boy in the cloud-boat, Makani-kau in his shell-boat, and the three girls in the spirit-boat.

The girls were carried to Oahu, and there found the shell-girl, Pupu-kani-oi, left by Makani-kau on his way to Lehua. They took her with her husband and his sisters in the spirit-boat. There were nine in the company of travellers to Hawaii: Kawelona in his cloud-boat; two girls from Kauai; Kaiahe, a girl from Oahu; three from Molokai, one from Maui; and a girl called Lihau. Makani-kau himself was the leader; he had taken the girls away. On this journey he turned their boats to Kahoolawe to visit Ka-moho-alii, the ruler of the sharks. There Makani-kau appeared in his finest human body, and they all landed. Makani-kau took Kawelona from his cloud-boat, went inland, and placed him in the midst of the company, telling them he was the husband for Lau-ka-ieie. They were all made welcome by the ruler of the sharks.

Ka-moho-alii called his sharks to bring food from all the islands over which they were placed as guardians; so they quickly brought prepared food, fish, flowers, leis, and gifts of all kinds.

The company feasted and rested. Then Ka-
moho-alii called his sharks to guard the travellers
on their journey. Makani-kau went in his shell-
boat, Kawelona in his cloud-boat, and they
were all carried over the sea until they landed
under the mountains of Hawaii.

Makani-kau, in his wind body, carried the boats
swiftly on their journey to Waipio. Lau-ka-ieie
heard her brother's voice calling her from the
sea. Hina answered. Makani-kau and Kawelona went up to Waimea to cross over to Lau-
ka-ieie's house, but were taken by Hina to the
top of Mauna Kea. Poliahu and Lilinoe saw
the two fine young men and called to them, but
Makani-kau passed by, without a word, to his
own wonderful home in the caves of the mountains resting in the heart of mists and fogs, and
placed all his travellers there. Makani-kau went
down to the sea and called the sharks of Ka-
moho-alii. They appeared in their human bodies
in the valley of Waipio, leaving their shark bodies
resting quietly in the sea. They feasted and
danced near the ancient temple of Kahuku-welo-
welo, which was the place where the wonderful
shell, Kiha-pu, was kept.

Makani-kau put seven shells on the top of the
precipice and they blew until sweet sounds floated
over all the land. Thus was the marriage of
Lau-ka-ieie and Kawelona celebrated.

All the shark people rested, soothed by the music. After the wedding they bade farewell and returned to Kahoolawe, going around the southern side of the island, for it was counted bad luck to turn back. They must go straight ahead all the way home. Makani-kau went to his sister's house, and met the girls and Lau-ka-ieie. He told her that his house was full of strangers, as the people of the different kupua bodies had assembled to celebrate the wedding. These were the kupua people of the Hawaiian Islands. The eepa people were more like fairies and gnomes, and were usually somewhat deformed. The kupuas may be classified as follows:

Ka-poe-kino-lau (the people who had leaf bodies).
   "   "   " -pua (the people who had flower bodies).
   "   "   " -manu (the people who had bird bodies).
   "   "   " -laau (trees of all kinds, ferns, vines, etc.).
   "   "   " -pupu (all shells).
   "   "   " -ao (all clouds).
   "   "   " -makani (all winds).
Ka-poe-kina-ia (all fish).
   "   "   " -mano (all sharks).
   "   "   " -limu (all sea-mosses).
   "   "   " -pokaku (all peculiar stones).
   "   "   " -hiwa-hiwa (all dangerous places of the pali).

After the marriage, Pupu-kani-oi (the singing shell) and her husband entered the shell-boat, and started back to Molokai. On their way they

heard sweet bird voices. Makani-kau had a
feather house covered with rainbow colors.
Later he went to Kauai, and brought back the
adopted parents of Kawelona to dwell on Hawaii,
where Lau-ka-ieie lived happily with her husband.

Hiilawe became very ill, and called his brother
Makani-kau and his sister Lau-ka-ieie to come
near and listen. He told them that he was
going to die, and they must bury him where he
could always see the eyes of the people, and then
he would change his body into a wonderful new
body.

The beautiful girl took his malo and leis and
placed them along the sides of the valley, where
they became trees and clinging vines, and Hina
made him live again; so Hiilawe became an
aumakua of the waterfalls. Makani-kau took
the body in his hands and carried it in the thunder
and lightning, burying it on the brow of the highest precipice of the valley. Then his body was
changed into a stone, which has been lying there
for centuries; but his ghost was made by Hina
into a kupua, so that he could always appear as
the wonderful misty falls of Waipio, looking into
the eyes of his people.

After many years had passed Hina assumed
permanently the shape of the beautiful ohia-tree,
making her home in the forest around the volcanoes of Hawaii. She still had magic power,

and was worshipped under the name Hina-ula-ohia. Makani-kau watched over Lau-ka-ieie, and when the time came for her to lay aside her human body she came to him as a slender, graceful woman, covered with leaves, her eyes blazing like fire. Makani-kau said: "You are a vine; you cannot stand alone. I will carry you into the forest and place you by the side of Hina. You are the ieie vine. Climb trees! Twine your long leaves around them! Let your blazing red flowers shine between the leaves like eyes of fire! Give your beauty to all the ohia-trees of the forest!"

Carried hither and thither by Makani-kau (great wind), and dropped by the side of splendid tall trees, the ieie vine has for centuries been one of the most graceful tree ornaments in all the forest life of the Hawaiian Islands.

Makani-kau in his spirit form blew the golden clouds of the islands into the light of the sun, so that the Rainbow Maiden, Anuenue, might lend her garments to all her friends of the ancient days.

VII

KAUHUHU, THE SHARK–GOD OF MOLOKAI

HE story of the shark-god Kauhuhu has been told under the legend of "Aikanaka (Man-eater)," which was the ancient name of the little harbor Pukoo, which lies at the entrance to one of the beautiful valleys of the island of Molokai. The better way is to take the legend as revealing the great man-eater in one of his most kindly aspects. The shark-god appears as the friend of a priest who is seeking revenge for the destruction of his children. Kamalo was the name of the priest. His heiau, or temple, was at Kaluaaha, a village which faced the channel between the islands of Molokai and Maui. Across the channel the rugged red-brown slopes of the mountain Eeke were lost in the masses of clouds which continually hung around its sharp peaks. The two boys of the priest delighted in the glorious revelations of sunrise and sunset tossed in shattered fragments of cloud color, and rejoiced in the reflected tints which danced to them over the swift channel-currents. It is no wonder that the courage of sky and sea entered into the hearts

of the boys, and that many deeds of daring were
done by them. They were taught many of the
secrets of the temple by their father, but were
warned that certain things were sacred to the
gods and must not be touched. The high chief,
or alii, of that part of the island had a temple a
short distance from Kaluaaha, in the valley of
the harbor which was called Aikanaka. The
name of this chief was Kupa. The chiefs always
had a house built within the temple walls as
their own residence, to which they could retire
at certain seasons of the year. Kupa had two
remarkable drums which he kept in his house at
the heiau. His skill in beating his drums was so
great that they could reveal his thoughts to the
waiting priests.

One day Kupa sailed far away over the sea
to his favorite fishing-grounds. Meanwhile the
boys were tempted to go to Kupa's heiau and try
the wonderful drums. The valley of the little
harbor Aikanaka bore the musical name Mapu-
lehu. Along the beach and over the ridge hastened the two sons of Kamalo. Quickly they
entered the heiau, found the high chief's house,
took out his drums and began to beat upon them.
Some of the people heard the familiar tones of
the drums. They dared not enter the sacred
doors of the heiau, but watched until the boys
became weary of their sport and returned home.

When Kupa returned they told him how the boys had beaten upon his sacred drums. Kupa was very angry, and ordered his mu, or temple sacrifice seekers, to kill the boys and bring their bodies to the heiau to be placed on the altar. When the priest Kamalo heard of the death of his sons, in bitterness of heart he sought revenge. His own power was not great enough to cope with his high chief; therefore he sought the aid of the seers and prophets of highest repute throughout Molokai. But they feared Kupa the chief, and could not aid him, and therefore sent him on to another kaula, or prophet, or sent him back to consult some one the other side of his home. All this time he carried with him fitting presents and sacrifices, by which he hoped to gain the assistance of the gods through their priests. At last he came to the steep precipice which overlooks Kalaupapa and Kalawao, the present home of the lepers. At the foot of this precipice was a heiau, in which the great shark-god was worshipped. Down the sides of the precipice he climbed and at last found the priest of the shark-god. The priest refused to give assistance, but directed him to go to a great cave in the bold cliffs south of Kalawao. The name of the cave was Anaopuhi, the cave of the eel. Here dwelt the great shark-god Kauhuhu and his guardians or watchers, Waka and Mo-o, the great dragons or reptiles

of Polynesian legends. These dragons were
mighty warriors in the defence of the shark-god,
and were his kahus, or caretakers, while he slept,
or when his cave needed watching during his
absence.

Kamalo, tired and discouraged, plodded along
through the rough lava fragments piled around
the entrance to the cave. He bore across his
shoulders a black pig, which he had carried many
miles as an offering to whatever power he could
find to aid him. As he came near to the cave
the watchmen saw him and said:—

"E, here comes a man, food for the great
[shark] Mano. Fish for Kauhuhu." But Kamalo came nearer and for some reason aroused
sympathy in the dragons. "E hele! E hele!"
they cried to him. "Away, away! It is death
to you. Here's the tabu place." "Death it
may be—life it may be. Give me revenge for
my sons—and I have no care for myself." Then
the watchmen asked about his trouble and he
told them how the chief Kupa had slain his sons
as a punishment for beating the drums. Then
he narrated the story of his wanderings all over
Molokai, seeking for some power strong enough
to overcome Kupa. At last he had come to the
shark-god—as the final possibility of aid. If
Kauhuhu failed him, he was ready to die; indeed
he had no wish to live. The mo-o assured him of

their kindly feelings, and told him that it was a very good thing that Kauhuhu was away fishing, for if he had been home there would have been no way for him to go before the god without suffering immediate death. There would have been not even an instant for explanations. Yet they ran a very great risk in aiding him, for they must conceal him until the way was opened by the favors of the great gods. If he should be discovered and eaten before gaining the aid of the shark-god, they, too, must die with him. They decided that they would hide him in the rubbish pile of taro peelings which had been thrown on one side when they had pounded taro. Here he must lie in perfect silence until the way was made plain for him to act. They told him to watch for the coming of eight great surf waves rolling in from the sea, and then wait in his place of concealment for some opportunity to speak to the god because he would come in the last great wave. Soon the surf began to roll in and break against the cliffs.

Higher and higher rose the waves until the eighth reared far above the waters and met the winds from the shore which whipped the curling crest into a shower of spray. It raced along the water and beat far up into the cave, breaking into foam, out of which the shark-god emerged. At once he took his human form and walked around the cave. As he passed the rubbish heap he cried out: "A man is here. I smell him." The dragons earnestly denied that any one was there, but the shark-god said, "There is surely a man in this cave. If I find him, dead men you are. If I find him not, you shall live." Then Kauhuhu looked along the walls of the cave and into all the hiding-places, but could not find him. He called with a loud voice, but only the echoes answered, like the voices of ghosts. After a thorough search he was turning away to attend to other matters when Kamalo's pig squealed. Then the giant shark-god leaped to the pile of taro leavings and thrust them apart. There lay Kamalo and the black pig which had been brought for sacrifice.

"Oh, the anger of the god!

Oh, the blazing eyes!"

Kauhuhu instantly caught Kamalo and lifted him from the rubbish up toward his great mouth. Now the head and shoulders are in Kauhuhu's mouth. So quickly has this been done that Kamalo has had no time to think. Kamalo speaks quickly as the teeth are coming down upon him. "E Kauhuhu, listen to me. Hear my prayer. Then perhaps eat me." The shark-god is astonished and does not bite. He takes Kamalo from his mouth and says: "Well for you that you spoke quickly. Perhaps you have a good thought. Speak." Then Kamalo told about his sons and their death at the hands of the executioners of the great chief, and that no one dared avenge him, but that all the prophets of the different gods had sent him from one place to another but could give him no aid. Sure now was he that Kauhuhu alone could give him aid. Pity came to the shark-god as it had come to his dragon watchers when they saw the sad condition of Kamalo. All this time Kamalo had held the hog which he had carried with him for sacrifice. This he now offered to the shark-god. Kauhuhu, pleased and compassionate, accepted the offering, and said: "E Kamalo. If you had come for any other purpose I would eat you, but your cause is sacred. I will stand as your kahu, your guardian, and sorely punish the high chief Kupa."

Then he told Kamalo to go to the heiau of the priest who told him to see the shark-god, take this priest on his shoulders, carry him over the steep precipices to his own heiau at Kaluaaha, and there live with him as a fellow-priest. They were to build a tabu fence around the heiau and put up the sacred tabu staffs of white tapa cloth. They must collect black pigs by the four hundred, red fish by the four hundred, and white chickens by the four hundred. Then they were to wait patiently for the coming of Kauhuhu. It was to be a strange coming. On the island Lanai, far to the west of the Maui channel, they should see a small cloud, white as snow, increasing until it covered the little island. Then that cloud would cross the channel against the wind and climb the mountains of Molokai until it rested on the highest peaks over the valley where Kupa had his temple. "At that time," said Kauhuhu, "a great rainbow will span the valley. I shall be in the care of that rainbow, and you may clearly understand that I am there and will speedily punish the man who has injured you. Remember that because you came to me for this sacred cause, therefore I have spared you, the only man who has ever stood in the presence of the shark-god and escaped alive." Swiftly did Kamalo go up and down precipices and along the rough hard ways to the heiau of the priest of the shark-god. Gladly did he carry him up from Kalaupapa to the mountain-ridge above. Quickly did he carry him to his home and there provide for him while he gathered together the black pigs, the red fish, and the white chickens within the sacred enclosure he had built. Here he brought his family, those who had the nearest and strongest claims upon him. When his work was done, his eyes burned with watching the clouds of the little western island Lanai. Ah, the days passed by so slowly! The weeks and the months came, so the legends say, and still Kamalo waited in patience. At last one day a white cloud appeared. It was unlike all the other white clouds he had anxiously watched during the dreary months. Over the channel it came. It spread over the hillsides and climbed the mountains and rested at the head of the valley belonging to Kupa. Then the watchers saw the glorious rainbow and knew that Kauhuhu had come according to his word.

The storm arose at the head of the valley. The winds struggled into a furious gale. The clouds gathered in heavy black masses, dark as midnight, and were pierced through with terrific flashes of lightning. The rain fell in floods, sweeping the hillside down into the valley, and rolling all that was below onward in a resistless mass toward the ocean. Down came the torrent upon the heiau belonging to Kupa, tearing its walls into fragments and washing Kupa and his people into the harbor at the mouth of the valley. Here the shark-god had gathered his people. Sharks filled the bay and feasted upon Kupa and his followers until the waters ran red and all were destroyed. Hence came the legendary name for that little harbor—Aikanaka, the place for man-eaters.

It is said in the legends that "when great clouds gather on the mountains and a rainbow spans the valley, look out for furious storms of wind and rain which come suddenly, sweeping down the

valley." It also said in the legends that this
strange storm which came in such awful power
upon Kupa spread out over the adjoining low-
lands, carrying great destruction everywhere,
but it paused at the tabu staff of Kamalo, and
rushed on either side of the sacred fence, not daring to touch any one who dwelt therein. Therefore Kamalo and his people were spared. The
legend has been called "Aikanaka" because of the
feast of the sharks on the human flesh swept down
into that harbor by the storm, but it seems more
fitting to name the story after the shark-god
Kauhuhu, who sent mighty storms and wrought
great destruction.

SHARK

VIII

THE SHARK–MAN OF WAIPIO VALLEY

THIS is a story of Waipio Valley, the most beautiful of all the valleys of the Hawaiian Islands, and one of the most secluded. It is now, as it has always been, very difficult of access. The walls are a sheer descent of over a thousand feet. In ancient times a narrow path slanted along the face of the bluffs wherever foothold could be found. In these later days the path has been enlarged, and horse and rider can descend into the valley's depths. In the upper end of the valley is a long silver ribbon water falling fifteen hundred feet from the brow of a precipice over which a mountain torrent swiftly hurls itself to the fertile valley below. Other falls show the convergence of several mountain streams to the ocean outlet offered by the broad plains of Waipio.

Here in the long ago high chiefs dwelt and sacred temples were built. From Waipio Valley Moikeha and Laa-Mai-Kahiki sailed away on their famous voyages to distant foreign lands. In this valley dwelt the priest who in the times of Maui was said to have the winds of heaven concealed in his calabash. Raising the cover a little, he sent gentle breezes in the direction of the open-ing. Severe storms and hurricanes were granted by swiftly opening the cover widely and letting a chaotic mass of fierce winds escape. The stories of magical powers of bird and fish as well as of the strange deeds of powerful men are almost innumerable. Not the least of the history-myths of Waipio Valley is the story of Nanaue, the shark-man, who was one of the cannibals of the ancient time.

Ka-moho-alii was the king of all the sharks which frequent Hawaiian waters. When he chose to appear as a man he was always a chief of dignified, majestic appearance. One day, while swimming back and forth just beneath the sur-face of the waters at the mouth of the valley, he saw an exceedingly beautiful woman coming to bathe in the white surf.

That night Ka-moho-alii came to the beach black with lava sand, crawled out of the water, and put on the form of a man. As a mighty chief he walked through the valley and mingled with the people. For days he entered into their sports and pastimes and partook of their bounty, al-ways looking for the beautiful woman whom he had seen bathing in the surf. When he found her he came to her and won her to be his wife.

Kalei was the name of the woman who married the strange chief. When the time came for a child to be born to them, Ka-moho-alii charged Kalei to keep careful watch of it and guard its body continually from being seen of men, and never allow the child to eat the flesh of any animal. Then he disappeared, never permitting Kalei to have the least suspicion that he was the king of the sharks.

When the child was born, Kalei gave to him the name "Nanaue." She was exceedingly surprised to find an opening in his back. As the child grew to manhood the opening developed into a large shark-mouth in rows of fierce sharp teeth.

From infancy to manhood Kalei protected Nanaue by keeping his back covered with a fine kapa cloak. She was full of fear as she saw Nanaue plunge into the water and become a shark. The mouth on his back opened for any kind of prey. But she kept the terrible birthmark of her son a secret hidden in the depths of her own heart.

For years she prepared for him the common articles of food, always shielding him from the temptation to eat meat. But when he became a man his grandfather took him to the men's eating-house, where his mother could no longer protect him. Meats of all varieties were given to him in great abundance, yet he always wanted more. His appetite was insatiable.

While under his mother's care he had been

taken to the pool of water into which the great
Waipio Falls poured its cascade of water.   There
he bathed, and, changing himself into a shark,
caught the small fish which were playing around
him.   His mother was always watching him to
give an alarm if any of the people came near to
the bathing-place.

As he became a man he avoided his companions
in all bathing and fishing.   He went away by
himself.   When the people were out in the deep
sea bathing or fishing, suddenly a fierce shark
would appear in their midst, biting and tearing
their limbs and dragging them down in the deep
water.   Many of the people disappeared secretly,
and great terror filled the homes of Waipio.

Nanaue's mother alone was certain that he was
the cause of the trouble.   He was becoming very
bold in his depredations.   Sometimes he would
ask when his friends were going out in the sea;
then he would go to a place at some distance,
leap into the sea, and swiftly dash to intercept
the return of his friends to the shore.   Perhaps
he would allay suspicion by appearing as a man
and challenge to a swimming-race.   Diving suddenly, he would in an instant become a shark and
destroy his fellow-swimmer.

The people felt that he had some peculiar power,
and feared him.   One day, when their high chief
had called all the men of the valley to prepare

the taro patches for their future supply of food, a fellow-workman standing by the side of Nanaue tore his kapa cape from his shoulders. The men behind cried out, "See the great shark-mouth!" All the people came running together, shouting, "A shark-man!" "A shark-man!"

Nanaue became very angry and snapped his shark-teeth together. Then with bitter rage he attacked those standing near him. He seized one by the arm and bit it in two. He tore the flesh of another in ragged gashes. Biting and snapping from side to side he ran toward the sea.

The crowd of natives surrounded him and blocked his way. He was thrown down and tied. The mystery had now passed from the valley. The people knew the cause of the troubles through which they had been passing, and all crowded around to see this wonderful thing, part man and part shark.

The high chief ordered their largest oven to be prepared, that Nanaue might be placed therein and burned alive. The deep pit was quickly cleaned out by many willing hands, and, with much noise and rejoicing, fire was placed within and the stones for heating were put in above the fire. "We are ready for the shark-man," was the cry.

During the confusion Nanaue quietly made his plans to escape. Suddenly changing himself to a shark, the cords which bound him fell off and he rolled into one of the rivers which flowed from the falls in the upper part of the valley.

None of the people dared to spring into the water for a hand-to-hand fight with the monster. They ran along the bank, throwing stones at Nanaue and bruising him. They called for spears that they might kill him, but he made a swift rush to the sea and swam away, never again to return to Waipio Valley.

Apparently Nanaue could not live long in the ocean. The story says that he swam over to the island of Maui and landed near the village Hana. There he dwelt for some time, and married a chiefess. Meanwhile he secretly killed and ate some of the people. At last his appetite for human flesh made him so bold that he caught a beautiful young girl and carried her out into the deep waters. There he changed himself into a shark and ate her body in the sight of the people.

The Hawaiians became very angry. They launched their canoes, and, throwing in all kinds of weapons, pushed out to kill their enemy. But he swam swiftly away, passing around the island until at last he landed on Molokai.

Again he joined himself to the people, and again one by one those who went bathing and fishing disappeared. The priests (kahunas) of the people at last heard from their fellow-priests of the island of Maui that there was a dangerous shark-man roaming through the islands. They sent warning to the people, urging all trusty fishermen to keep strict watch. At last they saw Nanaue change himself into a great fish. The fishermen waged a fierce battle against him. They entangled him in their nets, they pierced him with spears and struck him with clubs until the waters were red with his blood. They called on the gods of the sea to aid them. They uttered prayers and incantations. Soon Nanaue lost strength and could not throw off the ropes which were tied around him, nor could he break the nets in which he was entangled.

The fishermen drew him to the shore, and the people dragged the great shark body up the hill Puu-mano. Then they cut the body into small pieces and burned them in a great oven.

Thus died Nanaue, whose cannibal life was best explained by giving to him in mythology the awful appetite of an insatiable man-eating shark.

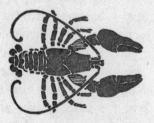

IX

THE STRANGE BANANA SKIN

KUKALI, according to the folk-lore of Hawaii, was born at Kalapana, the most southerly point of the largest island of the Hawaiian group. Kukali lived hundreds of years ago in the days of the migrations of Polynesians from one group of islands to another throughout the length and breadth of the great Pacific Ocean. He visited strange lands, now known under the general name, Kahiki, or Tahiti. Here he killed the great bird Halulu, found the deep bottomless pit in which was a pool of the fabled water of life, married the sister of Halulu, and returned to his old home. All this he accomplished through the wonderful power of a banana skin.

Kukali's father was a priest, or kahuna, of great wisdom and ability, who taught his children how to exercise strange and magical powers. To Kukali he gave a banana with the impressive charge to preserve the skin whenever he ate the fruit, and be careful that it was always under his control. He taught Kukali the wisdom of the makers of canoes and also how to select the fine-grained lava for stone knives and hatchets, and fashion the blade to the best shape. He instructed the young man in the prayers and incantations of greatest efficacy and showed him charms which would be more powerful than any charms his enemies might use in attempting to destroy him, and taught him those omens which were too powerful to be overcome. Thus Kukali became a wizard, having great confidence in his ability to meet the craft of the wise men of distant islands.

Kukali went inland through the forests and up the mountains, carrying no food save the banana which his father had given him. Hunger came, and he carefully stripped back the skin and ate the banana, folding the skin once more together. In a little while the skin was filled with fruit. Again and again he ate, and as his hunger was satisfied the fruit always again filled the skin, which he was careful never to throw away or lose.

The fever of sea-roving was in the blood of the Hawaiian people in those days, and Kukali's heart burned within him with the desire to visit the far-away lands about which other men told marvelous tales and from which came strangers like to the Hawaiians in many ways.

After a while he went to the forests and selected trees approved by the omens, and with many prayers fashioned a great canoe in which to embark upon his journey. The story is not told of the days passed on the great stretches of water as he sailed on and on, guided by the sun in the day and the stars in the night, until he came to the strange lands about which he had dreamed for years.

His canoe was drawn up on the shore and he lay down for rest. Before falling asleep he secreted his magic banana in his malo, or loin-cloth, and then gave himself to deep slumber. His rest was troubled with strange dreams, but his weariness was great and his eyes heavy, and he could not arouse himself to meet the dangers which were swiftly surrounding him.

A great bird which lived on human flesh was the god of the land to which he had come. The name of the bird was Halulu. Each feather of its wings was provided with talons and seemed to be endowed with human powers. Nothing like this bird was ever known or seen in the beautiful Hawaiian Islands. But here in the mysterious foreign land it had its deep valley, walled in like the valley of the Arabian Nights, over which the great bird hovered looking into the depths for food. A strong wind always attended the coming of Halulu when he sought the valley for his victims.

Kukali was lifted on the wings of the bird-god and carried to this hole and quietly laid on the ground to finish his hour of deep sleep.

When Kukali awoke he found himself in the shut-in valley with many companions who had been captured by the great bird and placed in this prison hole. They had been without food and were very weak. Now and then one of the number would lie down to die. Halulu, the bird-god, would perch on a tree which grew on the edge of the precipice and let down its wing to sweep across the floor of the valley and pick up the victims lying on the ground. Those who were strong could escape the feathers as they brushed over the bottom and hide in the crevices in the walls, but day by day the weakest of the prisoners were lifted out and prepared for Halulu's feast.

Kukali pitied the helpless state of his fellow-prisoners and prepared his best incantations and prayers to help him overcome the great bird. He took his wonderful banana and fed all the people until they were very strong. He taught them how to seek stones best fitted for the manufacture of knives and hatchets. Then for days they worked until they were all well armed with sharp stone weapons.

While Kukali and his fellow-prisoners were making preparation for the final struggle, the bird-god had often come to his perch and put his wing down into the valley, brushing the feathers back and forth to catch his prey.

Frequently the search was fruitless. At last he became very impatient, and sent his strongest feathers along the precipitous walls, seeking for victims.

Kukali and his companions then ran out from their hiding-places and fought the strong feathers, cutting them off and chopping them into small pieces.

Halulu cried out with pain and anger, and sent feather after feather into the prison. Soon one wing was entirely destroyed. Then the other wing was broken to pieces and the bird-god in his insane wrath put down a strong leg armed with great talons. Kukali uttered mighty invocations and prepared sacred charms for the protection of his friends.

After a fierce battle they cut off the leg and destroyed the talons. Then came the struggle with the remaining leg and claws, but Kukali's friends had become very bold. They fearlessly gathered around this enemy, hacking and pulling until the bird-god, screaming with pain, fell into the pit among the prisoners, who quickly cut the body into fragments.

The prisoners made steps in the walls, and by the aid of vines climbed out of their prison. When they had fully escaped, they gathered great piles of branches and trunks of trees and threw them into the prison until the body of the bird-

god was covered. Fire was thrown down and
Halulu was burned to ashes. Thus Kukali taught
by his charms that Halulu could be completely
destroyed.

But two of the breast feathers of the burning
Halulu flew away to his sister, who lived in a great
hole which had no bottom. The name of this
sister was Namakaeha. She belonged to the
family of Pele, the goddess of volcanic fires, who
had journeyed to Hawaii and taken up her home
in the crater of the volcano Kilauea.

Namakaeha smelled smoke on the feathers
which came to her, and knew that her brother was
dead. She also knew that he could have been
conquered only by one possessing great magical
powers. So she called to his people: "Who is the
great kupua [wizard] who has killed my brother?
Oh, my people, keep careful watch."

Kukali was exploring all parts of the strange
land in which he had already found marvelous
adventures. By and by he came to the great
pit in which Namakaeha lived. He could not
see the bottom, so he told his companions he was
going down to see what mysteries were concealed
in this hole without a bottom. They made a rope
of the hau* tree bark. Fastening one end around
his body he ordered his friends to let him down.
Uttering prayers and incantations he went down

* Paritium tiliaceus.

and down until, owing to counter incantations of Namakaeha's priests, who had been watching, the rope broke and he fell.

Down he went swiftly, but, remembering the prayer which a falling man must use to keep him from injury, he cried, "O Ku! guard my life!"

In the ancient Hawaiian mythology there was frequent mention of "the water of life." Sometimes the sick bathed in it and were healed. Sometimes it was sprinkled upon the unconscious, bringing them back to life. Kukali's incantation was of great power, for it threw him into a pool of the water of life and he was saved.

One of the kahunas (priests) caring for Namakaeha was a very great wizard. He saw the wonderful preservation of Kukali and became his friend. He warned Kukali against eating anything that was ripe, because it would be poison, and even the most powerful charms could not save him.

Kukali thanked him and went out among the people. He had carefully preserved his wonderful banana skin, and was able to eat apparently ripe fruit and yet be perfectly safe.

The kahunas of Namakaeha tried to overcome him and destroy him, but he conquered them, killed those who were bad, and entered into friendship with those who were good.

At last he came to the place where the great

chiefess dwelt. Here he was tested in many ways. He accepted the fruits offered him, but always ate the food in his magic banana. Thus he preserved his strength and conquered even the chiefess and married her. After living with her for a time he began to long for his old home in Hawaii. Then he persuaded her to do as her relative Pele had already done, and the family, taking their large canoe, sailed away to Hawaii, their future home.

X

THE OLD MAN OF THE MOUNTAIN

This is not a Hawaiian legend. It was written to show the superstitions of the Hawaiians, and in that respect it is accurate and worthy of preservation.

FAR away in New England one of the rugged mountain-sides has for many years been marked with the profile of a grand face. A noble brow, deep-set eyes, close-shut lips, Roman nose, and chin standing in full relief against a clear sky, made a landmark renowned throughout the country. The story is told of a boy who lived in the valley from which the face of the Old Man of the Mountain could be most clearly seen. As the years passed, the boy grew into a man of sterling character. When at last death came and the casket opened to receive the body of an old man, universally revered, the friends saw the likeness to the stone features of the Old Man of the Mountain, and recognized the source of the inspiration which had made one life useful and honored.

Near Honolulu, just beyond one of the great sugar plantations, is a ledge of lava deposited centuries ago. The lava was piled up into mountains, now dissolved into slopes of the richest sugar-land in the world. And yet sometimes the hard lava, refusing to disintegrate, thrusts itself out from the hillsides in ledges of grotesque form.

On one of these ancient lava ridges was the outline of an old man's face, to which the Hawaiians have given the name, "The Old Man of the Mountain." The laborers on the sugar-plantations, the passengers on the railroad trains, and the natives who still cling to their scattered homes sometimes have looked with superstitious awe upon the face made without hands. In the days gone by they have called it the "Akuapohaku" (the stone god). Shall we hear the story of Kamakau, who at some time in the indefinite past dwelt in the shadow of the stone face?

Kamakau means "the afraid." His name came to him as a child. He was a shrinking, sensitive, imaginative little fellow. He was surrounded by influences which turned his imagination into the paths of most unwholesome superstition. But beyond the beliefs of most of his fellows, in his own nature he was keenly appreciative of mysterious things. There was a spirit voice in every wind rustling the tops of the trees. Spirit faces appeared in unnum-

bered caricatures of human outline whenever
he lay on the grass and watched the sunlight
sift between the leaves. Everything he looked
upon or heard assumed some curious form
of life. The clouds were most mysterious of all,
for they so frequently piled up mass upon mass
of grandeur, in such luxurious magnificence and
such prodigal display of color, that his power
of thought lost itself in his almost daily dream
of some time wandering in the shadow valleys of
the precipitous mountains of heaven. Here he
saw also strangely symmetrical forms of man and
bird and fish. Sometimes cloud forests outlined
themselves against the blue sky, and then again
at times separated by months and even years, the
lights of the volcano-goddess, Pele, glorified her
path as she wandered in the spirit land, flashing
from cloud-peak to cloud-peak, while the thunder
voices of the great gods rolled in mighty volumes
of terrific impressiveness. Even in the night
Kamakau felt that the innumerable stars were
the eyes of the aumakuas (the spirits of the ancestors). It was not strange that such a child
should continually think that he saw spirit forms
which were invisible to his companions. It is no
wonder that he fancied he heard voices of the
menehunes (fairies), which his companions could
never understand. As he shrunk from places
where it seemed to him the spirits dwelt, his

companions called him "Kamakau," "the afraid."
When he grew older he necessarily became keenly
alive to all objects of Hawaiian superstition. He
never could escape the overwhelming presence of
the thousand and more gods which were supposed
to inhabit the Hawaiian land and sea. The omens
drawn from sacrifices, the voices from the bamboo dwelling-places of the oracles, the chants of
the prophets, and powers of praying to death he
accepted with unquestioning faith.

Two men were hunting in the forests of the
mountains of Oahu. Tired with the long chase
after the oo, the bird with the rare yellow feathers
from which the feather cloaks of the highest
chiefs were made, they laid aside spears and
snares and lay down for a rest. "I want the
valley of the stone god," said one: "its fertile
fields would make just the increase needed for my
retainers, and the 'moi,' the king, would give me
the land if Kamakau were out of the way."

"Are there any other members of his family,
O Inaina, who could resist your claim?"

"No, my friend Kokua. He is the only important chief in the valley."

"Pray him to death," was Kokua's sententious
advice.

"Good; I'll do it," said Inaina: "he is one who
can easily be prayed to death. 'The Afraid'
will soon die."

"If you will give me the small fish-pond nearest my own coral fish-walls I will be your messenger," said Kokua.

"Ah, that also is good," replied Inaina, after a moment's thought. "I will give you the small pond, and you must give the small thoughts, the hints, to his friends that powerful priests are praying Kamakau to death. All this must be very mysterious. No name can be mentioned, and you and I must be Kamakau's good friends."

It must be remembered that land tenure in ancient Hawaii was almost the same as that of the European feudal system. Occupancy depended upon the will of the high chief. He gave or took away at his own pleasure. The under-chiefs held the land as if it belonged to them, and were seldom troubled as long as the wishes of the high chief, or king, were carried out. Inaina felt secure in the use of his present property, and believed that he could easily find favor and obtain the land held by the Kamakau family if Kamakau himself could be removed. Without much further conference the two hunters returned to their homes. Inaina at once sought his family priest and stated his wish to have Kamakau prayed to death. They decided that the first step should be taken that night. It was absolutely necessary that something which had been a part of the body of Kamakau should be obtained. The priest appointed his confidential hunter of sacrifices to undertake this task. This servant of the temple was usually sent out to find human sacrifices to be slain and offered before the great gods on special occasions. As the darkness came on he crept near the grass house of Kamakau and watched for an opportunity of seizing what he wanted. The two most desired things in the art of praying to death were either a lock of hair from the head of the victim or a part of the spittle, usually well guarded by the trusted retainers who had charge of the spittoon.

It chanced to be "Awa night" for Kamakau, and the chief, having drunk heavily of the drug, had thrown himself on a mat and rolled near the grass walls. With great ingenuity the hunter of sacrifices located the chief and worked a hole through the thatch. Then with his sharp bone knife he sawed off a large lock of Kamakau's hair. When this was done he was about to creep away, but a native came near. Instantly grunting like a hog, he worked his way into the darkness. He saw outlined against the sky in the hands of the native the chief's spittoon. In a moment the hunter of sacrifices saw his opportunity. His past training in lying in wait and capturing men for sacrifice stood him in good stead at this time. The unsuspecting spittoon-carrier was seized by the throat and quickly strangled. The spittoon in falling from the retainer's hand had not been overturned. Exultant at his success, the hunter of sacrifices sped away in the darkness and placed his trophies in the hands of the priest. The next morning there was a great outcry in Kamakau's village. The dead body was found as soon as dawn crept over the valley, and the hand-polished family calabash was completely lost. When the people went to Kamakau's house with the report of the death of his retainer, they soon saw that the head of their chief had been dishonored. A great feeling of fear took possession of the village. Kamakau's priest hurried to the village temple to utter prayers and incantations against the enemy who had committed such an outrage.

Kokua soon heard the news and came to comfort his neighbor. After the greeting, "Auwe! auwe!" (Alas! alas!) Kokua said: "This is surely praying to death, and the gods have already given you over into the hands of your enemy. You will die. Very soon you will die." Soon Inaina and other chiefs came with their retainers. Among high and low the terrible statement was whispered: "Kamakau is being prayed to death, and no man knows his enemy." Many a strong man has gone to a bed of continued illness, and some have crossed the dark valley into the land of death, even in these days of enlightened civilization, simply frightened into the illness or death by the strong statements of friends and acquaintances. Such is the make-up of the minds of men that they are easily affected by the mysterious suggestions of others. It is purely a matter of mind-murder.

It is no wonder that in the days of the long ago Kamakau, moved by the terror of his friends and horrible suggestions of his two enemies, soon felt a great weakness conquering him. His natural disposition, his habit of seeing and hearing gods and spirits in everything around him, made it easy for him to yield to the belief that he was being prayed to death. His strength left him. He could take no food. A strange paralysis seemed to take possession of him. Mind and body were almost benumbed. He was really in the hands of unconscious mesmerists, who were putting him into a magnetic sleep, from which he was never expected to awake. It is a question to be answered only when all earthly problems have been solved. How many of the people prayed to death have really been dissected and prepared for burial while at first under mesmeric influences! The people gathered around Kamakau's thatched house. They thought that he would surely die before the next morning dawned. Inaina and Kokua were lying on the grass under the shade of a great candlenut-tree, quietly talking about the speedy success of their undertaking. A little girl was playing near them. It was Kamakau's little Aloha. This was all the name so far given to her. She was "My Aloha," "my dear one," to both father and mother. She heard a word uttered incautiously. Inaina had spoken with the accent of success and his voice was louder than he thought. He said, "We have great strength if we kill Kamakau." The child fled to her father. She found him in the half-unconscious state already described. She shook him. She called to him. She pulled his hands, and covered his face with kisses. Her tears poured over his hot, dry skin. Kamakau was aroused by the shock. He sat up, forgetting all the expectation of death.

Out through the doorway he glanced toward the west. The sinking sun was sending its most glorious beams into the grand clouds, while just beneath, reflecting the glory, lay the Old Man of the Mountain. The stone face was magnificent in its setting. The unruffled brow, the never-closing eyes, the firm lips, stood out in bold relief against the glory which was over and beyond them. Kamakau caught the inspiration. It seemed to his vivid imagination as if ten thousand good spirits were gathered in the heavens to fight for him. He leaped to his feet, strength came back into the wearied muscles, a new will-power took possession of him, and he cried: "I will not die! I will not die! The stone god is more powerful than the priests who pray to death!" His will had broken away from its chains, and, unfettered from all fear, Kamakau went forth to greet the wondering people and take up again the position of influence held among the chiefs of Oahu. The lesson is still needed in these beautiful ocean-bound islands that praying to death means either the use of poison or the attempt to terrify the victim by strong mental forces enslaving the will. In either case the aroused will is powerful in both resistance and watchfulness.

Feather Helmet

XI

HAWAIIAN GHOST TESTING

MANOA VALLEY for centuries has been
to the Hawaiians the royal palace of
rainbows. The mountains at the head
of the valley were gods whose children were the
divine wind and rain from whom was born the
beautiful rainbow-maiden who plays in and
around the valley day and night whenever misty
showers are touched by sunlight or moonlight.

The natives of the valley usually give her the
name of Kahalaopuna, or The Hala of Puna.
Sometimes, however, they call her Kaikawahine
Anuenue, or The Rainbow Maiden. The rainbow, the anuenue, marks the continuation of the
legendary life of Kahala.

The legend of Kahala is worthy of record in itself, but connected with the story is a very interesting account of an attempt to discover and
capture ghosts according to the methods supposed to be effective by the Hawaiian witch
doctors or priests of the long, long ago.

The legends say that the rainbow-maiden had
two lovers, one from Waikiki, and one from
Kamoiliili, half-way between Manoa and Waikiki.

Both wanted the beautiful arch to rest over their homes, and the maiden, the descendant of the gods, to dwell therein.

Kauhi, the Waikiki chief, was of the family of Mohoalii, the shark-god, and partook of the shark's cruel nature. He became angry with the rainbow-maiden and killed her and buried the body, but her guardian god, Pueo, the owl, scratched away the earth and brought her to life. Several times this occurred, and the owl each time restored the buried body to the wandering spirit. At last the chief buried the body deep down under the roots of a large koa-tree. The owl-god scratched and pulled, but the roots of the tree were many and strong. His claws were entangled again and again. At last he concluded that life must be extinct and so deserted the place.

The spirit of the murdered girl was wandering around hoping that it could be restored to the body, and not be compelled to descend to Milu, the Under-world of the Hawaiians. Po was sometimes the Under-world, and Milu was the god ruling over Po. The Hawaiian ghosts did not go to the home of the dead as soon as they were separated from the body. Many times, as when rendered unconscious, it was believed that the spirit had left the body, but for some reason had been able to come back into it and enjoy life among friends once more.

Kahala, the rainbow-maiden, was thus restored several times by the owl-god, but with this last failure it seemed to be certain that the body would grow cold and stiff before the spirit could return. The spirit hastened to and fro in great distress, trying to attract attention.

If a wandering spirit could interest some one to render speedy aid, the ancient Hawaiians thought that a human being could place the spirit back in the body. Certain prayers and incantations were very effective in calling the spirit back to its earthly home. The Samoans had the same thought concerning the restoration of life to one who had become unconscious, and had a special prayer, which was known as the prayer of life, by which the spirit was persuaded to return into its old home. The Hervey Islanders also had this same conception of any unconscious condition. They thought the spirit left the body but when persuaded to do so returned and brought the body back to life. They have a story of a woman who, like the rainbow-maiden, was restored to life several times.

The spirit of Kahala was almost discouraged. The shadows of real death were encompassing her, and the feeling of separation from the body was becoming more and more permanent. At last she saw a noble young chief approaching.

He was Mahana, the chief of Kamoiliili. The spirit hovered over him and around him and tried to impress her anguish upon him.

Mahana felt the call of distress, and attributed it to the presence of a ghost, or aumakua, a ghost-god. He was conscious of an influence leading him toward a large koa-tree. There he found the earth disturbed by the owl-god. He tore aside the roots and discovered the body bruised and disfigured and yet recognized it as the body of the rainbow-maiden whom he had loved.

In the King Kalakaua version of the story Mahana is represented as taking the body, which was still warm, to his home in Kamoiliili.

Mahana's elder brother was a kahuna, or witch-doctor, of great celebrity. He was called at once to pronounce the prayers and invocations necessary for influencing the spirit and the body to reunite. Long and earnestly the kahuna practised all the arts with which he was acquainted and yet completely failed. In his anxiety he called upon the spirits of two sisters who, as aumakuas, watched over the welfare of Mahana's clan. These spirit-sisters brought the spirit of the rainbow-maiden to the bruised body and induced it to enter the feet. Then, by using the forces of spirit-land, while the kahuna chanted and used his charms, they pushed the spirit of Kahala slowly up the body until "the soul was once more restored to its beautiful tenement."

The spirit-sisters then aided Mahana in restoring the wounded body to its old vigor and beauty. Thus many days passed in close comradeship between Kahala and the young chief, and they learned to care greatly for one another.

But while Kauhi lived it was unsafe for it to be known that Kahala was alive. Mahana determined to provoke Kauhi to personal combat; therefore he sought the places which Kauhi frequented for sport and gambling. Bitter words were spoken and fierce anger aroused until at last, by the skilful use of Kahala's story, Mahana led Kauhi to admit that he had killed the rainbow-maiden and buried her body.

Mahana said that Kahala was now alive and visiting his sisters.

Kauhi declared that if there was any one visiting Mahana's home it must be an impostor. In his anger against Mahana he determined a more awful death than could possibly come from any personal conflict. He was so sure that Kahala was dead that he offered to be baked alive in one of the native imus, or ovens, if she should be produced before the king and the principal chiefs of the district. Akaaka, the grandfather of Kahala, one of the mountain-gods of Manoa Valley, was to be one of the judges.

This proposition suited Mahana better than a conflict, in which there was a possibility of losing his own life.

Kauhi now feared that some deception might be practised. His proposition had been so eagerly accepted that he became suspicious; therefore he consulted the sorcerers of his own family. They agreed that it was possible for some powerful kahuna to present the ghost of the murdered maiden and so deceive the judges. They decided that it was necessary to be prepared to test the ghosts.

If it could be shown that ghosts were present, then the aid of "spirit catchers" from the land of Milu could be invoked. Spirits would seize these venturesome ghosts and carry them away to the spirit-land, where special punishments should be meted out to them. It was supposed that "spirit catchers" were continually sent out by Milu, king of the Under-world.

How could these ghosts be detected? They would certainly appear in human form and be carefully safeguarded. The chief sorcerer of Kauhi's family told Kauhi to make secretly a thorough test. This could be done by taking the large and delicate leaves of the ape*-plant and spreading them over the place where Kahala must walk and sit before the judges. A human being could not touch these leaves so carefully

* Gunnera petaloides.

placed without tearing and bruising them. A
ghost walking upon them could not make any
impression. Untorn leaves would condemn
Mahana to the ovens to be baked alive, and the
spirit catchers would be called by the sorcerers
to seize the escaped ghost and carry it back to
spirit-land. Of course, if some other maid of the
islands had pretended to be Kahala, that could
be easily determined by her divine ancestor
Akaaka. The trial was really a test of ghosts,
for the presence of Kahala as a spirit in her former
human likeness was all that Kauhi and his chief
sorcerer feared. The leaves were selected with
great care and secretly placed so that no one
should touch them but Kahala. There was
great interest in this strange contest for a home
in a burning oven. The imus had been prepared:
the holes had been dug, and the stones and wood
necessary for the sacrifice laid close at hand.

The king and judges were in their places. The
multitude of retainers stood around at a respect-
ful distance. Kauhi and his chief sorcerer were
placed where they could watch closely every
movement of the maiden who should appear
before the judgment-seat.

Kahala, the rainbow-maiden, with all the
beauty of her past girlhood restored to her,
drew near, attended by the two spirit-sisters
who had saved and protected her. The spirits

knew at once the ghost test by which Kahala
was to be tried. They knew also that she had
nothing to fear, but they must not be discovered.
The test applied to Kahala would only make more
evident the proof that she was a living human
being, but that same test would prove that they
were ghosts, and the spirit-catchers would be
called at once and they would be caught and
carried away for punishment. The spirit-sisters
could not try to escape. Any such attempt would
arouse suspicion and they would be surely seized.
The ghost-testing was a serious ordeal for Kahala
and her friends.

The spirit-sisters whispered to Kahala, telling
her the purpose attending the use of the ape
leaves and asking her to break as many of them
on either side of her as she could without at-
tracting undue attention. Thus she could aid
her own cause and also protect the sister-spirits.
Slowly and with great dignity the beautiful
rainbow-maiden and her friends passed through
the crowds of eager attendants to their places
before the king. Kahala bruised and broke as
many of the leaves as she could quietly. She
was recognized at once as the child of the divine
rain and wind of Manoa Valley. There was no
question concerning her bodily presence. The
torn leaves afforded ample and indisputable
testimony.

Kauhi, in despair, recognized the girl whom he had several times tried to slay. In bitter disappointment at the failure of his ghost-test the chief sorcerer, as the Kalakaua version of this legend says, "declared that he saw and felt the presence of spirits in some manner connected with her." These spirits, he claimed, must be detected and punished.

A second form of ghost-testing was proposed by Akaaka, the mountain-god. This was a method frequently employed throughout all the islands of the Hawaiian group. It was believed that any face reflected in a pool or calabash of water was a spirit face. Many times had ghosts been discovered in this way. The face in the water had been grasped by the watcher, crushed between his hands, and the spirit destroyed.

The chief sorcerer eagerly ordered a calabash of water to be quickly brought and placed before him. In his anxiety to detect and seize the spirits who might be attending Kahala he forgot about himself and leaned over the calabash. His own spirit face was the only one reflected on the surface of the water. This spirit face was believed to be his own true spirit escaping for the moment from the body and bathing in the liquid before him. Before he could leap back and restore his spirit to his body Akaaka leaped forward, thrust his hands down into the water and seized and crushed this spirit face between his mighty hands. Thus it was destroyed before it could return to its home of flesh and blood.

The chief sorcerer fell dead by the side of the calabash by means of which he had hoped to destroy the friends of the rainbow-maiden.

In this trial of the ghosts the two most powerful methods of making a test as far as known among the ancient Hawaiians were put in practice.

Kauhi was punished for his crimes against Kahala. He was baked alive in the imu prepared on his own land at Waikiki. His lands and retainers were given to Kahala and Mahana.

The story of Kahala and her connection with the rainbows and waterfalls of Manoa Valley has been told from time to time in the homes of the nature-loving native residents of the valley.

XII

HOW MILU BECAME THE KING OF GHOSTS

LONO was a chief living on the western side of the island Hawaii. He had a very red skin and strange-looking eyes. His choice of occupation was farming. This man had never been sick. One time he was digging with the oo, a long sharp-pointed stick or spade. A man passed and admired him. The people said, "Lono has never been sick." The man said, "He will be sick."

Lono was talking about that man and at the same time struck his oo down with force and cut his foot. He shed much blood, and fainted, falling to the ground. A man took a pig, went after the stranger, and let the pig go, which ran to this man. The stranger was Kamaka, a god of healing. He turned and went back at the call of the messenger, taking some popolo fruit and leaves in his cloak. When he came to the injured man he asked for salt, which he pounded into the fruit and leaves and placed in coco cloth and bound it on the wound, leaving it a long time. Then he went away.

As he journeyed on he heard heavy breathing, and turning saw Lono, who said, "You have helped me, and so I have left my lands in the care of my friends, directing them what to do, and have hastened after you to learn how to heal other people."

The god said, "Lono, open your mouth!" This Lono did, and the god spat in his mouth, so that the saliva could be taken into every part of Lono's body. Thus a part of the god became a part of Lono, and he became very skilful in the use of all healing remedies. He learned about the various diseases and the medicines needed for each. The god and Lono walked together, Lono receiving new lessons along the way, passing through the districts of Kau, Puna, Hilo, and then to Hamakua.

The god said, "It is not right for us to stay together. You can never accomplish anything by staying with me. You must go to a separate place and give yourself up to healing people."

Lono turned aside to dwell in Waimanu and Waipio Valleys and there began to practise healing, becoming very noted, while the god Kamaka made his home at Ku-kui-haele.

This god did not tell the other gods of the medicines that he had taught Lono. One of the other gods, Kalae, was trying to find some way to kill Milu, and was always making him sick. Milu, chief of Waipio, heard of the skill of Lono. Some had been sick even to death, and Lono had healed them. Therefore Milu sent a messenger to Lono who responded at once, came and slapped Milu all over the body, and said: "You are not ill. Obey me and you shall be well."

Then he healed him from all the sickness inside the body caused by Kalae. But there was danger from outside, so he said: "You must build a ti-leaf house and dwell there quietly for some time, letting your disease rest. If a company should come by the house making sport, with a great noise, do not go out, because when you go they will come up and get you for your death. Do not open the ti leaves and look out. The day you do this you shall die."

Some time passed and the chief remained in the house, but one day there was the confused noise of many people talking and shouting around his house. He did not forget the command of Lono. Two birds were sporting in a wonderful way in the sky above the forest. This continued all day until it was dark.

Then another long time passed and again Waipio was full of resounding noises. A great bird appeared in the sky resplendent in all kinds of feathers, swaying from side to side over the valley, from the top of one precipice across to the top of another, in grand flights passing over the heads of the people, who shouted until the valley re-echoed with the sound.

Milu became tired of that great noise and could not patiently obey his physician, so he pushed aside some of the ti leaves of his house and looked out upon the bird. That was the time when the bird swept down upon the house, thrusting a claw under Milu's arm, tearing out his liver. Lono saw this and ran after the bird, but it flew swiftly to a deep pit in the lava on one side of the valley and dashed inside, leaving blood spread on the stones. Lono came, saw the blood, took it and wrapped it in a piece of tapa cloth and returned to the place where the chief lay almost dead. He poured some medicine into the wound and pushed the tapa and blood inside. Milu was soon healed.

The place where the bird hid with the liver of Milu is called to this day Ke-ake-o-Milu ("The liver of Milu"). When this death had passed away he felt very well, even as before his trouble.

Then Lono told him that another death threatened him and would soon appear. He must dwell in quietness.

For some time Milu was living in peace and quiet after this trouble. Then one day the surf of Waipio became very high, rushing from far out even to the sand, and the people entered

into the sport of surf-riding with great joy and
loud shouts. This noise continued day by day,
and Milu was impatient of the restraint and forgot the words of Lono. He went out to bathe
in the surf.

When he came to the place of the wonderful
surf he let the first and second waves go by,
and as the third came near he launched himself upon it while the people along the beach
shouted uproariously. He went out again into
deeper water, and again came in, letting the first
and second waves go first. As he came to the
shore the first and second waves were hurled
back from the shore in a great mass against the
wave upon which he was riding. The two
great masses of water struck and pounded Milu,
whirling and crowding him down, while the surf-
board was caught in the raging, struggling
waters and thrown out toward the shore. Milu
was completely lost in the deep water.

The people cried: "Milu is dead! The chief
is dead!" The god Kalae thought he had killed
Milu, so he with the other poison-gods went on
a journey to Mauna Loa. Kapo and Pua, the
poison-gods, or gods of death, of the island Maui,
found them as they passed, and joined the company. They discovered a forest on Molokai,
and there as kupua spirits, or ghost bodies, entered into the trees of that forest, so the trees

became the kupua bodies. They were the medicinal or poison qualities in the trees.

Lono remained in Waipio Valley, becoming
the ancestor and teacher of all the good healing
priests of Hawaii, but Milu became the ruler
of the Under-world, the place where the spirits of
the dead had their home after they were driven
away from the land of the living. Many people
came to him from time to time.

He established ghostly sports like those which
his subjects had enjoyed before death. They
played the game kilu with polished coconut
shells, spinning them over a smooth surface to
strike a post set up in the centre. He taught konane, a game commonly called "Hawaiian checkers," but more like the Japanese game of "Go."
He permitted them to gamble, betting all the
kinds of property found in ghost-land. They
boxed and wrestled; they leaped from precipices into ghostly swimming-pools; they feasted
and fought, sometimes attempting to slay each
other. Thus they lived the ghost life as they
had lived on earth. Sometimes the ruler was
forgotten and the ancient Hawaiians called the
Under-world by his name—Milu. The New
Zealanders frequently gave their Under-world
the name " Miru." They also supposed that
the ghosts feasted and sported as they had done
while living.

XIII

A VISIT TO THE KING OF GHOSTS

WHEN any person lay in an unconscious state, it was supposed by the ancient Hawaiians that death had taken possession of the body and opened the door for the spirit to depart. Sometimes if the body lay like one asleep the spirit was supposed to return to its old home. One of the Hawaiian legends weaves their deep-rooted faith in the spirit-world into the expressions of one who seemed to be permitted to visit that ghost-land and its king. This legend belonged to the island of Maui and the region near the village Lahaina. Thus was the story told:

Ka-ilio-hae (the wild dog) had been sick for days and at last sank into a state of unconsciousness. The spirit of life crept out of the body and finally departed from the left eye into a corner of the house, buzzing like an insect. Then he stopped and looked back over the body he had left. It appeared to him like a massive mountain. The eyes were deep caves, into which the ghost looked. Then the spirit became afraid and went outside and rested on the roof of the house. The people began to wail loudly and the ghost fled from the noise to a coconut-tree and perched like a bird in the branches. Soon he felt the impulse of the spirit-land moving him away from his old home. So he leaped from tree to tree and flew from place to place wandering toward Kekaa, the place from which the ghosts leave the island of Maui for their home in the permanent spirit-land—the Under-world.

As he came near this doorway to the spirit-world he met the ghost of a sister who had died long before, and to whom was given the power of sometimes turning a ghost back to its body again. She was an aumakua-ho-ola (a spirit making alive). She called to Ka-ilio-hae and told him to come to her house and dwell for a time. But she warned him that when her husband was at home he must not yield to any invitation from him to enter their house, nor could he partake of any of the food which her husband might urge him to eat. The home and the food would be only the shadows of real things, and would destroy his power of becoming alive again.

The sister said, "When my husband comes to eat the food of the spirits and to sleep the sleep of ghosts, then I will go with you and you shall see all the spirit-land of our island and see the king of ghosts."

The ghost-sister led Ka-ilio-hae into the place of whirlwinds, a hill where he heard the voices of many spirits planning to enjoy all the sports of their former life. He listened with delight and drew near to the multitude of happy spirits. Some were making ready to go down to the sea for the hee-nalu (surf-riding). Others were already rolling the ulu-maika (the round stone discs for rolling along the ground). Some were engaged in the mokomoko, or umauma (boxing), and the kulakulai (wrestling), and the honuhonu (pulling with hands), and the loulou (pulling with hooked fingers), and other athletic sports.

Some of the spirits were already grouped in the shade of trees, playing the gambling games in which they had delighted when alive. There was the stone konane-board (somewhat like checkers), and the puepue-one (a small sand mound in which was concealed some object), and the puhenehene (the hidden stone under piles of kapa), and the many other trials of skill which permitted betting.

Then in another place crowds were gathered around the hulas (the many forms of dancing). These sports were all in the open air and seemed to be full of interest.

There was a strange quality which fettered every new-born ghost: he could only go in the direction into which he was pushed by the hand of some stronger power. If the guardian of a ghost struck it on one side, it would move off in the direction indicated by the blow or the push until spirit strength and experience came and he could go alone. The newcomer desired to join in these games and started to go, but the sister slapped him on the breast and drove him away. These were shadow games into which those who entered could never go back to the substantial things of life.

Then there was a large grass house inside which many ghosts were making merry. The visitor wanted to join this great company, but the sister knew that, if he once was engulfed by this crowd of spirits in this shadow-land, her brother could never escape. The crowds of players would seize him like a whirlwind and he would be unable to know the way he came in or the way out. Ka-ilio-hae tried to slip away from his sister, but he could not turn readily. He was still a very awkward ghost, and his sister slapped him back in the way in which she wanted him to go.

An island which was supposed to float on the ocean as one of the homes of the aumakuas (the ghosts of the ancestors) had the same characteristics. The ghosts (aumakuas) lived on the shadows of all that belonged to the earth-life. It was said that a canoe with a party of young people landed on this island of dreams and for some time enjoyed the food and fruits and sports, but after returning to their homes could not receive the nourishment of the food of their former lives, and soon died. The legends taught that no ghost passing out of the body could return unless it made the life of the aumakuas tabu to itself.

Soon the sister led her brother to a great field, stone walled, in which were such fine grass houses as were built only for chiefs of the highest rank. There she pointed to a narrow passage-way into which she told her brother he must enter by himself.

"This," she said, "is the home of Walia, the high chief of the ghosts living in this place. You must go to him. Listen to all he says to you. Say little. Return quickly. There will be three watchmen guarding this passage. The first will ask you, 'What is the fruit [desire] of your heart?' You will answer, 'Walia.' Then he will let you enter the passage.

"Inside the walls of the narrow way will be the second watchman. He will ask why you come; again answer, 'Walia,' and pass by him.

"At the end of the entrance the third guardian stands holding a raised spear ready to strike. Call to him, 'Ka-make-loa' [The Great Death]. This is the name of his spear. Then he will ask what you want, and you must reply, 'To see the chief,' and he will let you pass.

"Then again when you stand at the door of the great house you will see two heads bending together in the way so that you cannot enter or see the king and his queen. If these heads can catch a spirit coming to see the king without knowing the proper incantations, they will throw that ghost into the Po-Milu [The Dark Spirit-world]. Watch therefore and remember all that is told you.

"When you see these heads, point your hands straight before you between them and open your arms, pushing these guards off on each side, then the ala-nui [the great way] will be open for you—and you can enter.

"You will see kahilis [soft long feather fans] moving over the chiefs. The king will awake and call, 'Why does this traveller come?' You will reply quickly, 'He comes to see the Divine One.' When this is said no injury will come to you. Listen and remember and you will be alive again."

Ka-ilio-hae did as he was told with the three watchmen, and each one stepped back, saying, "Noa" (the tabu is lifted), and he pushed by. At the door he shoved the two heads to the side and entered the chief's house to the ka-ikuwai (the middle), falling on his hands and knees. The servants were waving the kahilis this way and that. There was motion, but no noise.

The chief awoke, looked at Ka-ilio-hae, and said: "Aloha, stranger, come near. Who is the high chief of your land?"

Then Ka-ilio-hae gave the name of his king, and the genealogy from ancient times of the chiefs dead and in the spirit-world.

The queen of ghosts arose, and the kneeling spirit saw one more beautiful than any woman in all the island, and he fell on his face before her.

The king told him to go back and enter his body and tell his people about troubles near at hand.

While he was before the king twice he heard messengers call to the people that the sports were all over; any one not heeding would be thrown into the darkest place of the home of the ghosts when the third call had been sounded.

The sister was troubled, for she knew that at the third call the stone walls around the king's houses would close and her brother would be held fast forever in the spirit-land, so she uttered her incantations and passed the guard. Softly she called. Her brother reluctantly came. She seized him and pushed him outside. Then they heard the third call, and met the multitude of ghosts coming inland from their sports in the sea, and other multitudes hastening homeward from their work and sports on the land.

They met a beautiful young woman who called to them to come to her home, and pointed to a point of rock where many birds were resting. The sister struck her brother and forced him down to the seaside where she had her home and her responsibility, for she was one of the guardians of the entrance to the spirit-world.

She knew well what must be done to restore the spirit to the body, so she told her brother they must at once obey the command of the king; but the brother had seen the delights of the life of the aumakuas and wanted to stay. He tried to slip away and hide, but his sister held him fast and compelled him to go along the beach to his old home and his waiting body.

When they came to the place where the body lay she found a hole in the corner of the house and pushed the spirit through. When he saw the body he was very much afraid and tried to escape, but the sister caught him and pushed him inside the foot up to the knee. He did not like the smell of the body and tried to rush back, but she pushed him inside again and held the foot fast and shook him and made him go to the head.

The family heard a little sound in the mouth and saw breath moving the breast, then they knew that he was alive again. They warmed the body and gave a little food. When strength returned he told his family all about his wonderful journey into the land of ghosts.

Note.—A student should read next the articles "Homeless and Desolate Ghosts" and "Ancestor Ghost-Gods" in Part II.

XIV

KALAI–PAHOA, THE POISON–GOD

THE Bishop Museum of Honolulu has one of the best as well as one of the most scientifically arranged collections of Hawaiian curios in the world. In it are images of many of the gods of long ago. One of these is a helmeted head made of wicker-work, over which has been woven a thick covering of beautiful red feathers bordered with yellow feathers. This was the mighty war-god, Kukailimoku, of the great Kamehameha. Another is a squat rough image, crudely carved out of wood. This was Kamehameha's poison-god.

The ancient Hawaiians were acquainted with poisons of various kinds. They understood the medicinal qualities of plants and found some of these strong enough to cause sickness and even death. One of the Hawaiian writers said: "The opihi-awa is a poison shell-fish. These are bitter and deadly and can be used in putting enemies to death. Kalai-pahoa is also a tree in which there is the power to kill."

Kamehameha's poison-god was called Kalai-pahoa, because it was cut from that tree which grew in the upland forest on the island of Molokai.

A native writer says there was an antidote for the poison from Kalai-pahoa, and he thus describes it: "The war-god and the poison-god were not left standing in the temples like the images of other gods, but after being worshipped were wrapped in kapa and laid away.

"When the priest wanted Kalai-pahoa he was taken down and anointed with coconut-oil and wrapped in a fresh kapa cloth. Then he was set up above the altar and a feast prepared before him, awa to drink, and pig, fish, and poi to eat.

"Then the priest who had special care of this god would scrape off a little from the wood, and put it in an awa cup, and hold the cup before the god, chanting a prayer for the life of the king, the government, and the people. One of the priests would then take the awa cup, drink the contents, and quickly take food.

"Those who were watching would presently see a red flush creep over his cheeks, growing stronger and stronger, while the eyes would become glassy and the breath short like that of a dying man. Then the priest would touch his lips to the stick, Mai-ola, and have his life restored. Mai-ola was a god who had another tree. When Kalai-pahoa entered his tree on Molokai, Mai-ola

entered another tree and became the enemy of
the poison-god."

The priests of the poison-god were very powerful in the curious rite called pule-ana-ana, or
praying to death. The Hawaiians said: "Perhaps the priests of Kalai-pahoa put poison in
bananas or in taro. It was believed that they
scraped the body of the image and put the pieces
in the food of the one they wished to pray to
death. There was one chief who was very skilful
in waving kahilis, or feather fans, over any one
and shaking the powder of death into the food
from the moving feathers. Another would have
scrapings in his cloak and would drop them into
whatever food his enemy was eating." The
spirit of death was supposed to reside in the wood
of the poison-god.

A very interesting legend was told by the old
people to their children to explain the coming
of medicinal and poisonous properties into the
various kinds of trees and plants. These stories
all go back to the time when Milu died and became the king of ghosts. They say that after
the death of Milu the gods left Waipio Valley on
the island of Hawaii and crossed the channel to
the island Maui.

These gods had all kinds of power for evil, such
as stopping the breath, chilling or burning the
body, making headaches or pains in the stomach,

or causing palsy or lameness or other injuries, even inflicting death.

Pua and Kapo, who from ancient times have been worshipped as goddesses having medicinal power, joined the party when they came to Maui. Then all the gods went up Mauna Loa, a place where there was a large and magnificent forest with fine trees, graceful vines and ferns, and beautiful flowers. They all loved this place, therefore they became gods of the forest.

Near this forest lived Kane-ia-kama, a high chief, who was a very great gambler. He had gambled away all his possessions. While he was sleeping, the night of his final losses, he heard some one call, "O Kane-ia-kama, begin your play again." He shouted out into the darkness: "I have bet everything. I have nothing left."

Then the voice again said, "Bet your bones, bet your bones, and see what will happen."

When he went to the gambling-place the next day the people all laughed at him, for they knew his goods were all gone. He sat down among them, however, and said: "I truly have nothing left. My treasures are all gone, but I have my bones. If you wish, I will bet my body, then I will play with you."

The other chiefs scornfully placed some property on one side and said, "That will be of the same value as your bones."

They gambled and he won. The chiefs were angry at their loss and bet again and again. He always won until he had more wealth than any one on the island.

After the gambling days were over he heard again the same voice saying: "O Kane-ia-kama, you have done all that I told you and have become very rich in property and servants. Will you obey once more?"

The chief gratefully thanked the god for the aid that he had received, and said he would obey. The voice then said: "Perhaps we can help you to one thing. You are now wealthy, but there is a last gift for you. You must listen carefully and note all I show you."

Then this god of the night pointed out the trees into which the gods had entered when they decided to remain for a time in the forest, and explained to him all their different characteristics. He showed him where gods and goddesses dwelt and gave their names. Then he ordered Kane-ia-kama to take offerings of pigs, fish, coconuts, bananas, chickens, kapas, and all other things used for sacrifice, and place them at the roots of these trees into which the gods had entered, the proper offerings for each.

The next morning he went into the forest and saw that he had received a very careful description of each tree. He observed attentively the tree

shown as the home of the spirit who had become
his strange helper.

Before night fell he placed offerings as commanded. As a worshipper he took each one of
these trees for his god, so he had many gods of
plants and trees.

For some reason not mentioned in the legends
he sent woodcutters to cut down these trees, or
at least to cut gods out of them with their stone
axes.

They began to cut. The koko (blood) of the
trees, as the natives termed the flowing sap,
and the chips flying out struck some of the
woodcutters and they fell dead.

Kane-ia-kama made cloaks of the long leaves
of the ieie vine and tied them around his men,
so that their bodies could not be touched, then
the work was easily accomplished.

The chief kept these images of gods cut from
the medicinal trees and could use them as he
desired. The most powerful of all these gods was
that one whose voice he had heard in the night.
To this god he gave the name Kalai-pahoa (The-
one-cut-by-the-pahoa-or-stone-axe).

One account relates that the pahoa (stone)
from which the axe was made came from Kalakoi,
a celebrated place for finding a very hard lava of
fine grain, the very best for making stone
implements.

The god who had spoken to the chief in his dream was sometimes called Kane-kulana-ula (noted red Kane).

The gods were caught by the sacrifices of the chief while they were in their tree bodies before they could change back into their spirit bodies, therefore their power was supposed to remain in the trees.

It was said that when Kane-kulana-ula changed into his tree form he leaped into it with a tremendous flash of lightning, thus the great mana, or miraculous power, went into that tree.

The strange death which came from the god Kalai-pahoa made that god and his priest greatly feared. One of the pieces of this tree fell into a spring at Kaakee near the maika, or disc-rolling field, on Molokai. All the people who drank at that spring died. They filled it up and the chiefs ruled that the people should not keep branches or pieces of the tree for the injury of others. If such pieces were found in the possession of any one he should die. Only the carved gods were to be preserved.

Kahekili, king of Maui at the time of the accession of Kamehameha to the sovereignty of the island Hawaii, had these images in his possession as a part of his household gods.

Kamehameha sent a prophet to ask him for one of these gods. Kahekili refused to send

one, but told him to wait and he should have
the poison-god and the government over all the
islands.

One account records that a
small part from the poison
one was then given.

So, after the death of Kahekili, Kamehameha did conquer all the islands with their
hosts of gods, and Kalai-
pahoa, the poison-god, came
into his possession.

Kukailimoku

The overthrow of idolatry
and the destruction of the
system of tabus came in
1819, when most of the
wooden gods were burned or
thrown into ponds and rivers, but a few were
concealed by their caretakers. Among these
were the two gods now to be seen in the Bishop
Museum* in Honolulu.

* See Appendix.

XV

KE–AO–MELE–MELE, THE MAID OF THE GOLDEN CLOUD

THE Hawaiians never found gold in their islands. The mountains being of recent volcanic origin do not show traces of the precious metals; but hovering over the mountain-tops clustered the glorious golden clouds built up by damp winds from the seas. The Maiden of the Golden Cloud belonged to the cloud mountains and was named after their golden glow.

Her name in the Hawaiian tongue was Ke-ao-mele-mele (The Golden Cloud). She was said to be one of the first persons brought by the gods to find a home in the Paradise of the Pacific.

In the ancient times, the ancestors of the Hawaiians came from far-off ocean lands, for which they had different names, such as The Shining Heaven, The Floating Land of Kane, The Far-off White Land of Kahiki, and Kuai-he-lani. It was from Kuai-he-lani that the Maiden of the Golden Cloud was called to live in Hawaii.

In this legendary land lived Mo-o-inanea (self-reliant dragon). She cared for the first children of the gods, one of whom was named Hina, later known in Polynesian mythology as Moon Goddess.

Mo-o-inanea took her to Ku, one of the gods. They lived together many years and a family of children came to them.

Two of the great gods of Polynesia, Kane and Kanaloa, had found a beautiful place above Honolulu on Oahu, one of the Hawaiian Islands. Here they determined to build a home for the first-born child of Hina.

Thousands of eepa (gnome) people lived around this place, which was called Waolani. The gods had them build a temple which was also called Waolani (divine forest).

When the time came for the birth of the child, clouds and fogs crept over the land, thunder rolled and lightning flashed, red torrents poured down the hillsides, strong winds hurled the rain through bending trees, earthquakes shook the land, huge waves rolled inland from the sea. Then a beautiful boy was born. All these signs taken together signified the birth of a chief of the highest degree—even of the family of the gods.

Kane and Kanaloa sent their sister Anuenue (rainbow) to get the child of Ku and Hina that they might care for it. All three should be the caretakers.

Anuenue went first to the place where Mo-o-inanea dwelt, to ask her if it would be right. Mo-o-inanea said she might go, but if they brought up that child he must not have a wife from any of the women of Hawaii-nui-akea (great wide Hawaii).

Anuenue asked, "Suppose I get that child; who is to give it the proper name?"

Mo-o-inanea said: "You bring the child to our brothers and they will name this child. They have sent you, and the responsibility of the name rests on them."

Anuenue said good-by, and in the twinkling of an eye stood at the door of the house where Ku dwelt.

Ku looked outside and saw the bright glow of the rainbow, but no cloud or rain, so he called Hina. "Here is a strange thing. You must come and look at it. There is no rain and there are no clouds or mist, but there is a rainbow at our door."

They went out, but Anuenue had changed her rainbow body and stood before them as a very beautiful woman, wrapped only in the colors of the rainbow.

Ku and Hina began to shiver with a nameless terror as they looked at this strange maiden. They faltered out a welcome, asking her to enter their house.

As she came near to them Ku said, "From what place do you come?"

Anuenue said: "I am from the sky, a messenger sent by my brothers to get your child that they may bring it up. When grown, if the child wants its parents, we will bring it back. If it loves us it shall stay with us."

Hina bowed her head and Ku wailed, both thinking seriously for a little while. Then Ku said: "If Mo-o-inanea has sent you she shall have the child. You may take this word to her."

Anuenue replied: "I have just come from her and the word I brought you is her word. If I go away I shall not come again."

Hina said to Ku: "We must give this child according to her word. It is not right to disobey Mo-o-inanea."

Anuenue took the child and studied the omens for its future, then she said, "This child is of the very highest, the flower on the top of the tree."

She prepared to take the child away, and bade the parents farewell. She changed her body into the old rainbow colors shining out of a mist, then she wrapped the child in the rainbow, bearing it away.

Ku and Hina went out looking up and watching the cloud of rainbow colors floating in the sky. Strong, easy winds blew and carried this

cloud out over the ocean. The navel-string had
not been cut off, so Anuenue broke off part and
threw it into the ocean, where it became the
Hee-makoko, a blood-red squid. This is the
legendary origin of that kind of squid.

Anuenue passed over many islands, coming at
last to Waolani to the temple built by the
gnomes under Kane and Kanaloa. They con-
secrated the child, and cut off another part of
the navel-cord. Kanaloa took it to the Nuuanu
pali back of Honolulu, to the place called Ka-
ipu-o-Lono. Kane and Kanaloa consulted about
servants to live with the boy, and decided that
they must have only ugly ones, who would not
be desired as wives by their boy. Therefore
they gathered together the lame, crooked, deformed, and blind among the gnome people.
There were hundreds of these living in different
homes, and performing different tasks. Anuenue
was the ruler over all of them. This child was
named Kahanai-a-ke-Akua (the one adopted
by the gods). He was given a very high tabu
by Kane and Kanaloa. No one was allowed to
stand before him and no person's shadow could
fall upon him.

Hina again conceived. The signs of this child
appeared in the heavens and were seen on Oahu.
Kane wanted to send Lanihuli and Waipuhia,
their daughters, living near the pali of Waolani

and Nuuanu. The girls asked where they should go.

Kane said: "We send you to the land Kuai-he-lani, a land far distant from Hawaii, to get the child of Hina. If the parents ask you about your journey, tell them you have come for the child. Tell our names and refer to Mo-o-inanea. You must now look at the way by which to go to Kuai-he-lani.

They looked and saw a great bird—Iwa. They got on this bird and were carried far up in the heavens. By and by the bird called two or three times. The girls were frightened and looking down saw the bright shining land Kuai-he-lani below them. The bird took them to the door of Ku's dwelling-place.

Ku and Hina were caring for a beautiful girl-baby. They looked up and saw two fine women at their door. They invited them in and asked whence they came and why they travelled.

The girls told them they were sent by the gods Kane and Kanaloa. Suddenly a new voice was heard. Mo-o-inanea was by the house. She called to Ku and to Hina, telling them to give the child into the hands of the strangers, that they might take her to Waka, a great priestess, to be brought up by her in the ohia forests of the island of Hawaii. She named that girl Pali-ula, and explained to the parents that when

Paliula should grow up, to be married, the boy
of Waolani should be her husband. The girls
then took the babe. They were all carried by
the bird, Iwa, far away in the sky to Waolani,
where they told Kane and Kanaloa the message
or prophecy of Mo-o-inanea.

The gods sent Iwa with the child to Waka, on
Hawaii, to her dwelling-place in the districts
of Hilo and Puna where she was caring for all
kinds of birds in the branches of the trees and
among the flowers.

Waka commanded the birds to build a house
for Paliula. This was quickly done. She commanded the bird Iwa to go to Nuumea-lani, a
far-off land above Kuai-he-lani, the place where
Mo-o-inanea was now living.

It was said that Waka, by her magic power,
saw in that land two trees, well cared for by
multitudes of servants; the name of one was
"Makalei." This was a tree for fish. All
kinds of fish would go to it. The second was
"Kalala-ika-wai." This was the tree used for
getting all kinds of food. Call this tree and
food would appear.

Waka wanted Mo-o-inanea to send these trees
to Hawaii.

Mo-o-inanea gave these trees to Iwa, who
brought them to Hawaii and gave them to Waka.
Waka rejoiced and took care of them. The

bird went back to Waolani, telling Kane and Kanaloa all the journey from first to last.

The gods gave the girls resting-places in the fruitful lands under the shadow of the beautiful Nuuanu precipices.

Waka watched over Paliula until she grew up, beautiful like the moon of Mahea-lani (full moon).

The fish tree, Makalei, which made the fish of all that region tame, was planted by the side of running water, in very restful places spreading all along the river-sides to the seashore. Fish came to every stream where the trees grew, and filled the waters.

The other tree was planted and brought prepared food for Paliula. The hidden land where this place was has always been called Paliula, a beautiful green spot—a home for fruits and flowers and birds in a forest wilderness.

When Paliula had grown up, Waka went to Waolani to meet Kane, Kanaloa, and Anuenue. There she saw Kahanai-a-ke-Akua (the boy brought up by the gods) and desired him for Paliula's husband. There was no man so splendid and no woman so beautiful as these two. The caretakers decided that they must be husband and wife.

Waka returned to the island Hawaii to prepare for the coming of the people from Waolani.

Waka built new houses finer and better than the first, and covered them with the yellow feathers of the Mamo bird with the colors of the rainbow resting over. Anuenue had sent some of her own garments of rainbows.

Then Waka went again to Waolani to talk with Kane and Kanaloa and their sister Anuenue.

They said to her: "You return, and Anuenue will take Kahanai and follow. When the night of their arrival comes, lightning will play over all the mountains above Waolani and through the atmosphere all around the temple, even to Hawaii. After a while, around your home the leaves of the trees will dance and sing and the ohia-trees themselves bend back and forth shaking their beautiful blossoms. Then you may know that the Rainbow Maiden and the boy are by your home on the island of Hawaii.

Waka returned to her home in the tangled forest above Hilo. There she met her adopted daughter and told her about the coming of her husband.

Soon the night of rolling thunder and flashing lightning came. The people of all the region around Hilo were filled with fear. Kane-hekili (flashing lightning) was a miraculous body which Kane had assumed. He had gone before the boy and the rainbow, flashing his way through the heavens.

The gods had commanded Kane-hekili to dwell in the heavens in all places wherever the gods desired him to be, so that he could go wherever commanded. He always obeyed without questioning.

The thunder and lightning played over ocean and land while the sun was setting beyond the islands in the west.

After a time the trees bent over, the leaves danced and chanted their songs. The flowers made a glorious halo as they swayed back and forth in their dances.

Kane told the Rainbow Maiden to take their adopted child to Hawaii-nui-akea.

When she was ready, she heard her brothers calling the names of trees which were to go with her on her journey. Some of the legends say that Laka, the hula-god, was dancing before the two. The tree people stood before the Rainbow Maiden and the boy, ready to dance all the way to Hawaii. The tree people are always restless and in ceaseless motion. The gods told them to sing together and dance. Two of the tree people were women, Ohia and Lamakea. Lamakea is a native whitewood tree. There are large trees at Waialae in the mountains of the island Oahu. Ohia is a tree always full of fringed red blossoms. They were very beautiful in their wind bodies. They were kupuas, or wizards, and could be moving trees or dancing women as they chose.

The Rainbow Maiden took the boy in her arms up into the sky, and with the tree people went on her journey. She crossed over the islands to the mountains of the island Hawaii, then went down to find Paliula.

She placed the tree people around the house to dance and sing with soft rustling noises.

Waka heard the chants of the tree people and opened the door of the glorious house, calling for Kahanai to come in. When Paliula saw him, her heart fluttered with trembling delight, for she knew this splendid youth was the husband selected by Waka, the prophetess. Waka called the two trees belonging to Paliula to bring plenty of fish and food.

Then Waka and Anuenue left their adopted children in the wonderful yellow feather house.

The two young people, when left together, talked about their birthplaces and their parents. Paliula first asked Kahanai about his land and his father and mother. He told her that he was the child of Ku and Hina from Kuai-he-lani, brought up by Kane and the other gods at Waolani.

The girl went out and asked Waka about her parents, and learned that this was her first-born brother, who was to be her husband because they had very high divine blood. Their descendants would be the chiefs of the people. This marriage was a command from parents and ancestors and Mo-o-inanea.

She went into the house, telling the brother who she was, and the wish of the gods.

After ten days they were married and lived together a long time.

At last, Kahanai desired to travel all around Hawaii. In this journey he met Poliahu, the white-mantle girl of Mauna Kea, the snow-covered mountain of the island Hawaii.

Meanwhile, in Kuai-he-lani, Ku and Hina were living together. One day Mo-o-inanea called to Hina, telling her that she would be the mother of a more beautiful and wonderful child than her other two children. This child should live in the highest places of the heavens and should have a multitude of bodies which could be seen at night as well as in the day.

Mo-o-inanea went away to Nuumea-lani and built a very wonderful house in Ke-alohi-lani (shining land), a house always turning around by day and by night like the ever moving clouds, indeed, it was built of all kinds of clouds and covered with fogs. There she made a spring of flowing water and put it outside for the coming child to have as a bath. There she planted the seeds of magic flowers, Kanikawi and Kanikawa, legendary plants of old Hawaii. Then she went to Kuai-he-lani and found Ku and Hina asleep. She took a child out of the top of the head of Hina and carried it away to the new home, naming it Ke-ao-mele-mele (the yellow cloud), the Maiden of the Golden Cloud, a wonderfully beautiful girl.

No one with a human body was permitted to come to this land of Nuumea-lani. No kupuas were allowed to make trouble for the child.

The ao-opua (narrow-pointed clouds) were appointed watchmen serving Ke-ao-mele-mele, the Maiden of the Golden Cloud.

All the other clouds were servants: the ao-opua-kakahiaka (morning clouds), ao-opua-ahiahi (evening clouds), ao-opua-aumoe (night clouds), ao-opua-kiei (peeking clouds), ao-opua-aha-lo (down-looking clouds), ao-opua-ku (image-shaped clouds rising at top of sea), opua-hele (morning-flower clouds), opua-noho-mai (resting clouds), opua-mele-mele (gold-colored clouds), opua-lani (clouds high up), ka-pae-opua (at surface of sea or clouds along the horizon), ka-lani-opua (clouds up above horizon), ka-ma-kao-ka-lani (clouds in the eye of the sun), ka-wele-lau-opua (clouds highest in the sky).

All these clouds were caretakers watching for the welfare of that girl. Mo-o-inanea gave them their laws for service.

She took Ku-ke-ao-loa (the long cloud of Ku) and put him at the door of the house of clouds, with great magic power. He was to be the messenger to all the cloud-lands of the parents and ancestors of this girl.

"The Eye of the Sun" was the cloud with magic power to see all things passing underneath near or far.

Then there was the opua-alii, cloud-chief with the name Ka-ao-opua-ola (the sharp-pointed living cloud). This was the sorcerer and astronomer, never weary, never tired, knowing and watching over all things.

Mo-o-inanea gave her mana-nui, or great magic power, to Ke-ao-mele-mele—with divine tabus. She made this child the heir of all the divine islands, therefore she was able to know what was being done everywhere. She understood how the Kahanai had forsaken his sister to live with Poliahu. So she went to Hawaii to aid her sister Paliula.

When Mo-o-inanea had taken the child from the head of Hina, Ku and Hina were aroused. Ku went out and saw wonderful cloud images standing near the house, like men. Ku and Hina watched these clouds shining and changing colors in the light of the dawn, as the sun appeared. The light of the sun streamed over the skies. For three days these changing clouds

were around them. Then in the midst of these
clouds appeared a strange land of the skies surrounded by the ao-opua (the narrow-pointed
clouds). In the night of the full moon, the aka
(ghost) shadow of that land leaped up into the
moon and became fixed there. This was the
Alii-wahine-aka-malu (the queen of shadows),
dwelling in the moon.

Ku and Hina did not understand the meaning
of these signs or shadows, so they went back into
the house, falling into deep sleep.

Mo-o-inanea spoke to Hina in her dreams, saying that these clouds were signs of her daughter
born from the head—a girl having great knowledge and miraculous power in sorcery, who
would take care of them in their last days. They
must learn all the customs of kilo-kilo, or sorcery.

Mo-o-inanea again sent Ku-ke-ao-loa to the
house of Ku, that cloud appearing as a man at
their door.

They asked who he was. He replied: "I
am a messenger sent to teach you the sorcery or
witcheries of cloud-land. You must have this
knowledge that you may know your cloud-
daughter. Let us begin our work at this time."

They all went outside the house and sat down
on a stone at the side of the door.

Ku-ke-ao-loa looked up and called Mo-o-
inanea by name. His voice went to Ke-alohi-

lani, and Mo-o-inanea called for all the clouds
to come with their ruler Ke-ao-mele-mele.

> "Arise, O yellow cloud,
>   Arise, O cloud—the eye of the sun,
>   Arise, O beautiful daughters of the skies,
>   Shine in the eyes of the sun, arise!"

Ke-ao-mele-mele arose and put on her glorious
white kapas like the snow on Mauna Kea. At
this time the cloud watchmen over Kuai-he-lani
were revealing their cloud forms to Hina and Ku.
The Long Cloud told Hina and Ku to look
sharply into the sky to see the meaning of all the
cloud forms which were servants of the divine
chiefess, their habits of meeting, moving, sepa-
rating, their forms, their number, the stars appearing through them, the fixed stars and moving
clouds, the moving stars and moving clouds, the
course of the winds among the different clouds.

When he had taught Ku and Hina the sorcery
of cloud-land, he disappeared and returned to
Ke-alohi-lani.

Some time afterward, Ku went out to the side
of their land. He saw a cloud of very beautiful
form, appearing like a woman. This was resting
in the sky above his head. Hina woke up,
missed Ku, looked out and saw Ku sitting on
the beach watching the clouds above him. She
went to him and by her power told him that
he had the desire to travel and that he might

go on his journey and find the woman of his
vision.

A beautiful chiefess, Hiilei, was at that time
living in one of the large islands of the heavens.
Ku and Hina went to this place. Ku married
Hiilei, and Hina found a chief named Olopana
and married him. Ku and Hiilei had a red-
skin child, a boy, whom they named Kau-mai-
liula (twilight resting in the sky). This child
was taken by Mo-o-inanea to Ke-alohi-lani to
live with Ke-ao-mele-mele. Olopana and Hina
had a daughter whom they called Kau-lana-iki-
pokii (beautiful daughter of sunset), who was
taken by Ku and Hiilei.

Hina then called to the messenger cloud to
come and carry a request to Mo-o-inanea that
Kau-mai-liula be given to her and Olopana.
This was done. So they were all separated from
each other, but in the end the children were
taken to Hawaii.

Meanwhile Paliula was living above Hilo
with her husband Kahanai-a-ke-Akua (adopted
son of the gods). Kahanai became restless and
determined to see other parts of the land, so he
started on a journey around the islands. He soon
met a fine young man Waiola (water of life).

Waiola had never seen any one so glorious in
appearance as the child of the gods, so he fell
down before him, saying: "I have never seen

any one so divine as you. You must have come from the skies. I will belong to you through the coming years."

The chief said, "I take you as my aikane [bosom friend] to the last days."

They went down to Waiakea, a village near Hilo, and met a number of girls covered with wreaths of flowers and leaves. Kahanai sent Waiola to sport with them. He himself was of too high rank. One girl told her brother Kanuku to urge the chief to come down, and sent him leis. He said he could not receive their gift, but must wear his own lei. He called for his divine caretaker to send his garlands, and immediately the most beautiful rainbows wrapped themselves around his neck and shoulders, falling down around his body.

Then he came down to Waiakea. The chief took Kanuku also as a follower and went on up the coast to Hamakua.

The chief looked up Mauna Kea and there saw the mountain women, who lived in the white land above the trees. Poliahu stood above the precipices in her kupua-ano (wizard character), revealing herself as a very beautiful woman wearing a white mantle.

When the chief and his friends came near the cold place where she was sitting, she invited them to her home, inland and mountainward.

The chief asked his friends to go with him to the mountain house of the beauty of Mauna Kea.

They were well entertained. Poliahu called her sisters, Lilinoe and Ka-lau-a-kolea, beautiful girls, and gave them sweet-sounding shells to blow. All through the night they made music and chanted the stirring songs of the grand mountains. The chief delighted in Poliahu and lived many months on the mountain.

One morning Paliula in her home above Hilo awoke from a dream in which she saw Poliahu and the chief living together, so she told Waka, asking if the dream were true. Waka, by her magic power, looked over the island and saw the three young men living with the three maidens of the snow mantle. She called with a penetrating voice for the chief to return to his own home. She went in the form of a great bird and brought him back.

But Poliahu followed, met the chief secretly and took him up to Mauna Kea again, covering the mountain with snow so that Waka could not go to find them.

Waka and the bird friends of Paliula could not reach the mountain-top because of the cold. Waka went to Waolani and told Anuenue about Paliula's trouble.

Anuenue was afraid that Kane and Kanaloa might hear that the chief had forsaken his sister,

and was much troubled, so she asked Waka to
go with her to see Mo-o-inanea at Ke-alohi-lani,
but the gods Kane and Kanaloa could not
be deceived. They understood that there was
trouble, and came to meet them.

Kane told Waka to return and tell the girl to
be patient; the chief should be punished for
deserting her.

Waka returned and found that Paliula had
gone away wandering in the forest, picking·lehua
flowers on the way up toward the Lua Pele, the
volcano pit of Pele, the goddess of fire. There
she had found a beautiful girl and took her as
an aikane (friend) to journey around Hawaii.
They travelled by way of the districts of Puna,
Kau, and Kona to Waipio, where she saw a fine-
looking man standing above a precipice over
which leaped the wonderful mist-falls of Hiilawe.
This young chief married the beautiful girl
friend of Paliula.

Poliahu by her kupua power recognized
Paliula, and told the chief that she saw her with
a new husband.

Paliula went on to her old home and rested
many days. Waka then took her from island to
island until they were near Oahu. When they
came to the beach, Paliula leaped ashore and
went up to Manoa Valley. There she rushed
into the forest and climbed the ridges and preci-

pices. She wandered through the rough places,
her clothes torn and ragged.

Kane and Kanaloa saw her sitting on the
mountain-side. Kane sent servants to find her
and bring her to live with them at Waolani.
When she came to the home of the gods in
Nuuanu Valley she thought longingly of her
husband and sang this mele:

> " Lo, at Waolani is my lei of the blood-red rain,
>   The lei of the misty rain gathered and put together,
>   Put together in my thought with tears.
>   Spoiled is the body by love,
>   Dear in the eyes of the lover.
>   My brother, the first-born,
>   Return, oh, return, my brother."

Paliula, chanting this, turned away from Waolani to Waianae and dwelt for a time with the
chiefess Kalena.

While Paliula was living with the people of
the cold winds of Waianae she wore leis of
mokahana berries and fragrant grass, and was
greatly loved by the family. She went up the
mountain to a great gulch. She lay down to
sleep, but heard a sweet voice saying, "You
cannot sleep on the edge of that gulch." She
was frequently awakened by that voice. She
went on up the mountain-ridges above Waianae.
At night when she rested she heard the voices
again and again. This was the voice of Hii-lani-
wai, who was teaching the hula dance to the

girls of Waianae. Paliula wanted to see the
one who had such a sweet voice, so went along
the pali and came to a hula house, but the house
was closed tight and she could not look in.

She sat down outside. Soon Hii-lani-wai
opened the door and saw Paliula and asked her
to come in. It was the first time Paliula had
seen this kind of dancing. Her delight in the
dance took control of her mind, and she forgot
her husband and took Hii-lani-wai as her aikane,
dwelling with her for a time.

One day they went out into the forest. Kane
had sent the dancing trees from Waolani to
meet them. While in the forest they heard the
trees singing and dancing like human beings.
Hii-lani-wai called this a very wonderful thing.
Paliula told her that she had seen the trees do
this before. The trees made her glad.

They went down to the seaside and visited
some days. Paliula desired a boat to go to
the island of Kauai. The people told them of
the dangerous waters, but the girls were stub-
born, so they were given a very small boat.
Hii-lani-wai was steering, and Paliula was pad-
dling and bailing out the water. The anger of
the seas did not arise. On the way Paliula fell
asleep, but the boat swiftly crossed the channel.
Their boat was covered with all the colors of
the rainbow. Some women on land at last saw

them and beckoned with their hands for them
to come ashore.

Malu-aka (shadow of peace) was the most
beautiful of all the women on Kauai. She was
kind and hospitable and took them to her house.
The people came to see these wonderful strangers.
Paliula told Malu-aka her story. She rested,
with the Kauai girls, then went with Malu-aka
over the island and learned the dances of Kauai,
becoming noted throughout the island for her
wonderful grace and skill, dancing like the wind,
feet not touching the ground. Her songs and
the sound of the whirling dance were lifted by
the winds and carried into the dreams of Ke-ao-
mele-mele.

Meanwhile, Ke-ao-mele-mele was living with
her cloud-watchmen and Mo-o-inanea at Ke-
alohi-lani. She began to have dreams, hearing a
sweet voice singing and seeing a glorious woman
dancing, while winds were whispering in the
forests. For five nights she heard the song and
the sound of the dance. Then she told Mo-o-
inanea, who explained her dream, saying: "That
is the voice of Paliula, your sister, who is dancing and singing near the steep places of Kauai.
Her brother-husband has forsaken her and she
has had much trouble. He is living with Poliahu
on Hawaii."

When Ke-ao-mele-mele heard this, she thought

she would go and live with her sister. Mo-o-ina-nea approved of the thought and gave her all kinds of kupua power. She told her to go and see the god Kane, who would tell her what to do.

At last she started on her journey with her watching clouds. She went to see Hina and Olopana, and Ku and Hiilei. She saw Kau-mai-liula (twilight resting in the sky), who was very beautiful, like the deep red flowers of the ohia in the shadows of the leaves of the tree. She determined to come back and marry him after her journey to Oahu.

When she left Kuai-he-lani with her followers she flew like a bird over the waves of the sea. Soon she passed Niihau and came to Kauai to the place where Paliula was dancing, and as a cloud with her cloud friends spied out the land. The soft mists of her native land were scattered over the people by these clouds above them. Paliula was reminded of her birth-land and the loved people of her home.

Ke-ao-mele-mele saw the beauty of the dance and understood the love expressed in the chant. She flew away from Kauai, crossed the channel, came to Waolani, met Kane and Kanaloa and told them she had come to learn from them what was the right thing to do for the sister and the husband who had deserted her. Kane suggested a visit to Hawaii to see Paliula and the chief, so she flew over the islands to Hawaii. Then she went up the mountain with the ao-pii-kai (a cloud rising from the sea and climbing the mountain) until she saw Poliahu and her beautiful sisters.

Poliahu looked down the mountain-side and saw a woman coming, but she looked again and the woman had disappeared. In a little while a golden cloud rested on the summit of the mountain. It was the maid in her cloud body watching her brother and the girl of the white mountains. For more than twenty days she remained in that place. Then she returned to Waolani on Oahu.

Ke-ao-mele-mele determined to learn the hulas and the accompanying songs. Kane told her she ought to learn these things. There was a fine field for dancing at the foot of the mountain near Waolani, and Kane had planted a large kukui-tree by its side to give it shade.

Kane and his sister Anuenue went to this field and sat down in their place. The daughters of Nuuanu Pali were there. Kane sent Ke-ao-mele-mele after the dancing-goddess, Kapo, who lived at Mauna Loa. She was the sister of the poison-gods and knew the art of sorcery. Ke-ao-mele-mele took gifts, went to Kapo, made offerings, and thus for the first time secured a goddess for the hula.

Kapo taught Ke-ao-mele-mele the chants and the movements of the different hulas until she was very skilful. She flew over the seas to Oahu and showed the gods her skill. Then, she went to Kauai, danced on the surf and in the clouds and above the forests and in the whirlwinds. Each night she went to one of the other islands, danced in the skies and over the waters, and returned home. At last she went to Hawaii to Mauna Kea, where she saw Kahanai, her brother. She persuaded him to leave the maiden of the snow mantle and return to Waolani. Paliula and her friends had returned to the home with Waka, where she taught the leaves of clinging vines and the flowers and leaves on the tender swinging branches of the forest trees new motions in their dances with the many kinds of winds.

One day Kahanai saw signs among the stars and in the clouds which made him anxious to travel, so he asked Kane for a canoe. Kane called the eepa and the menehune people and told them to make canoes to carry Kahanai to his parents.

These boats were made in the forests of Waolani. When the menehunes finished their boat they carried it down Nuuanu Valley to Puunui. There they rested and many of the little folk came to help, taking the canoe down, step by step, to the mouth of the Nuuanu stream, where they had the aid of the river to the ocean.

The menehunes left the boat floating in the water and went back to Waolani. Of the fairy people it was said: "No task is difficult. It is the work of one hand."

On the way down Nuuanu Valley the menehunes came to Ka-opua-ua (storm cloud). They heard the shouting of other people and hurried along until they met the Namunawa people, the eepas, carrying a boat, pushing it down. When they told the eepas that the chief had already started on his journey with double canoes, the eepas left their boat there to slowly decay, but it is said that it lasted many centuries.

The people who made this boat were the second class of the little people living at Waolani, having the characters of human beings, yet having also the power of the fairy people. These were the men of the time of Kane and the gods.

Kahanai and his friends were in their boat when a strong wind swept down Nuuanu, carrying the dry leaves of the mountains and sweeping them into the sea. The waves were white as the boat was blown out into the ocean. Kahanai steered by magic power, and the boat like lightning swept away from the islands to the homes of Ku and Hina. The strong wind and the swift current were with the boat, and the voyage was through the waves like swift lightning flashing through clouds.

Ku and Hiilei saw the boat coming. Its signs were in the heavens. Ku came and asked the travellers, "What boat is this, and from what place has it come?"

Kahanai said, "This boat has come from Waolani, the home of the gods Kane and Kanaloa and of Ke-ao-mele-mele."

Then Ku asked again, "Whose child are you?"

He replied, "The son of Ku and Hina."

"How many other children in your family?"

He said: "There are three of us. I am the boy and there are two sisters, Paliula and Ke-ao-mele-mele. I have been sent by Ke-ao-mele-mele to get Kau-mai-liula and Kau-lana-iki-pokii to go to Oahu."

Ku and his wife agreed to the call of the messenger for their boy Kau-mai-liula.

When Kahanai saw him he knew that there was no other one so fine as this young man who quickly consented to go to Oahu with his servants.

Ku called for some beautiful red boats with red sails, red paddles,—everything red. Four good boatmen were provided for each boat, men who came from the land of Ulu-nui—the land of the yellow sea and the black sea of Kane— and obeyed the call of Mo-o-inanea. They had kupua power. They were relatives of Kane and Kanaloa.

The daughter of Hina and Olopana, Kaulana-iki-pokii, cried to go with her brother, but Mo-o-inanea called for her dragon family to make a boat for her and ordered one of the sorcerer dragons to go with her and guard her. They called the most beautiful shells of the sea to become the boats for the girl and her attendants. They followed the boats of Kahanai. With one stroke of the paddles the boats passed through the seas around the home of the gods. With the second stroke they broke through all the boundaries of the great ocean and with the third dashed into the harbor of old Honolulu, then known as Kou.

When the boats of Kahanai and Kau-mai-liula came to the surf of Mamala, there was great shouting inland of Kou, the voices of the eepas of Waolani. Mists and rainbows rested over Waolani. The menehunes gathered in great multitudes at the call of Kane, who had seen the boats approaching.

The menehune people ran down to lift up the boats belonging to the young chief. They made a line from Waolani to the sea. They lifted up the boats and passed them from hand to hand without any effort, shouting with joy.

While these chiefs were going up to Waolani,

Ke-ao-mele-mele came from Hawaii in her cloud boats.

Kane had told the menehunes to prepare houses quickly for her. It was done like the motion of the eye.

Ke-ao-mele-mele entered her house, rested, and after a time practised the hula.

The chiefs also had houses prepared, which they entered.

The shell boats found difficulty in entering the bay because the other boats were in the way. So they turned off to the eastern side of the harbor. Thus the ancient name of that side was given Ke-awa-lua (the second harbor, or the second landing-place in the harbor). Here they landed very quietly. The shell boats became very small and Kau-lana and her companions took them and hid them in their clothes. They went along the beach, saw some fish. The attendants took them for the girl. This gave the name Kau-lana-iki-pokii to that place to this day. As they went along, the dragon friend made the signs of a high chief appear over the girl. The red rain and arching bow were over her, so the name was given to that place, Ka-ua-koko-ula (blood rain), which is the name to this day.

The dragon changed her body and carried the girl up Nuuanu Valley very swiftly to the house of Ke-ao-mele-mele (the maiden of the golden cloud) without the knowledge of Kane and the others. They heard the hula of Ke-ao-mele-mele. Soon she felt that some one was outside, and looking saw the girl and her friend, with the signs of a chief over her.

So she called:

"Is that you, O eye of the day?
O lightning-like eye from Kahiki,
The remembered one coming to me.
The strong winds have been blowing,
Trembling comes into my breast,
A stranger perhaps is outside,
A woman whose sign is the fog,
A stranger and yet my young sister,
The flower of the divine home-land,
The wonderful land of the setting sun
Going down into the deep blue sea.
You belong to the white ocean of Kane,
You are Kau-lana-iki-pokii,
The daughter of the sunset,
The woman coming in the mist,
In the thunder and the flash of lightning
Quivering in the sky above.
Light falls on the earth below.
The sign of the chiefess,
The woman high up in the heavens,
Kau-lana-iki-pokii,
Enter, enter, here am I."

Those outside heard the call and understood that Ke-ao-mele-mele knew who they were. They entered and saw her in all the beauty of her high divine blood.

They kissed. Kau-lana told how she had come. Ke-ao-mele-mele told the dragon to go and stay on the mountain by the broken pali at the head of Nuuanu Valley. So she went to the precipice and became the watchman of that place. She was the first dragon on the islands. She watched with magic power. Later, Mo-o-inanea came with many dragons to watch over the islands. Ke-ao-mele-mele taught her young sister the different hulas and meles, so that they were both alike in their power.

When the young men heard hula voices in the other houses they thought they would go and see the dancers. At the hour of twilight Wao-lani shook as if in an earthquake, and there was thunder and lightning.

The young men and Anuenue went to the house and saw the girls dancing, and wondered how Kau-lana had come from the far-off land.

Ke-ao-mele-mele foretold the future for the young people. She told Kau-lana that she would never marry, but should have magic medicine power for all coming days, and Kahanai should have the power over all customs of priests and sorcerers and knowledge of sacrifices, and should be the bosom friend of the medicine-goddess. She said that they would all go to Waipio, Hawaii. Kane, Kanaloa, and Anuenue approved of her commands.

Ke-ao-mele-mele sent Kau-lana to Hawaii to tell Paliula to come and live with them at Waipio

and find Kahanai once more. Kau-lana hastened to Hawaii in her shell boat. She called,
"O my red shell boat of the deep blue sea and
the black sea, come up to me."

The shell boat appeared on the surface of the
sea, floating. The girl was carried swiftly to
Hawaii. There she found Waka and Paliula
and took them to Waipio. They lived for a
time there, then all went to Waolani to complete the marriage of Ke-ao-mele-mele to Kau-
mai-liula.

Kane sent Waka and Anuenue for Ku and
Hiilei, Hina and Olopana with Mo-o-inanea to
come to Oahu.

Mo-o-inanea prepared large ocean-going canoes
for the two families, but she and her people went
in their magic boats.

Mo-o-inanea told them they would never
return to these lands, but should find their future
home in Hawaii.

Waka went on Ku's boat, Anuenue was with
Hina. Ku and his friends looked back, the land
was almost lost; they soon saw nothing until the
mountains of Oahu appeared before them.

They landed at Heeia on the northern side of
the Nuuanu precipice, went over to Waolani,
and met all the family who had come before.

Before Mo-o-inanea left her land she changed
it, shutting up all the places where her family

had lived. She told all her kupua dragon family to come with her to the place where the gods had gone. Thus she made the old lands entirely different from any other lands, so that no other persons but gods or ghosts could live in them.

Then she rose up to come away. The land was covered with rainclouds, heavy and black. The land disappeared and is now known as "The Hidden Land of Kane."

She landed on Western Oahu, at Waialua, so that place became the home of the dragons, and it was filled with the dragons from Waialua to Ewa.

This was the coming of dragons to the Hawaiian Islands.

At the time of the marriage of Ke-ao-mele-mele and Kau-mai-liula, the Beautiful Daughter of Sunset came from the island Hawaii bringing the two trees Makalei and Makuukao, which prepared cooked food and fish. When she heard the call to the marriage she came with the trees. Makalei brought great multitudes of fish from all the ocean to the Koo-lau-poko side of the island Oahu. The ocean was red with the fish.

Makuukao came to Nuuanu Valley with Kau-lana, entered Waolani, and provided plenty of food.

Then Makalei started to come up from the sea.

Kau-lana-iki-pokii told the gods and people that there must not be any noise when that great tree came up from the sea. They must hear and remain silent.

When the tree began to come to the foot of the pali, the menehunes and eepas were astonished and began to shout with a great voice, for they thought this was a mighty kupua from Kahiki coming to destroy them.

When they had shouted, Makalei fell down at the foot of the pali near Ka-wai-nui, and lies there to this day. So this tree never came to Waolani and the fish were scattered around the island.

Kau-lana's wrath was very great, and he told Kane and the others to punish these noisy ones, to take them away from this wonderful valley of the gods. He said, "No family of these must dwell on Waolani." Thus the fairies and the gnomes were driven away and scattered over the islands.

For a long time the Maiden of the Golden Cloud and her husband, Twilight Resting in the Sky, ruled over all the islands even to the mysterious lands of the ocean. When death came they laid aside their human bodies and never made use of them again—but as aumakuas, or ghost-gods, they assumed their divine forms, and in the skies, over the mountains and valleys, they have appeared for hundreds of years watching over and cheering their descendants.

NOTE.—See now article on "Dragon Ghost-gods" in Part II.

XVI

PUNA AND THE DRAGON

TWO images of goddesses were clothed in yellow kapa cloth and worshipped in the temples. One was Kiha-wahine, a noted dragon-goddess, and the other was Haumea, who was also known as Papa, the wife of Wakea, a great ancestor-god among the Polynesians.

Haumea is said to have taken as her husband, Puna, a chief of Oahu. He and his people were going around the island. The surf was not very good, and they wanted to find a better place. At last they found a fine surf-place where a beautiful woman was floating on the sea.

She called to Puna, "This is not a good place for surf." He asked, "Where is there a place?" She answered, "I know where there is one, far outside." She desired to get Puna. So they swam way out in the sea until they were out of sight nor could they see the sharp peaks of the mountains. They forgot everything else but each other. This woman was Kiha-wahine.

The people on the beach wailed, but did not take canoes to help them. They swam over to Molokai. Here they left their surf-boards on the beach and went inland. They came to the cave house of the woman. He saw no man inside nor did he hear any voice, all was quiet.

Puna stayed there as a kind of prisoner and obeyed the commands of the woman. She took care of him and prepared his food. They lived as husband and wife for a long time, and at last his real body began to change.

Once he went out of the cave. While standing there he heard voices, loud and confused. He wanted to see what was going on, but he could not go, because the woman had laid her law on him, that if he went away he would be killed.

He returned to the cave and asked the woman, "What is that noise I heard from the sea?" She said: "Surf-riding, perhaps, or rolling the maika stone. Some one is winning and you heard the shouts." He said, "It would be fine for me to see the things you have mentioned." She said, "To-morrow will be a good time for you to go and see."

In the morning he went down to the sea to the place where the people were gathered together and saw many sports.

While he was watching, one of the men, Hinole, the brother of his wife, saw him and was pleased.

When the sports were through he invited Puna to go to their house and eat and talk.

Hinole asked him, "Whence do you come, and what house do you live in?" He said, "I am from the mountains, and my house is a cave." Hinole meditated, for he had heard of the loss of Puna at Oahu. He loved his brother-in-law, and asked, "How did you come to this place?" Puna told him all the story. Then Hinole told him his wife was a goddess. "When you return and come near to the place, go very easily and softly, and you will see her in her real nature, as a mo-o, or dragon; but she knows all that you are doing and what we are saying. Now listen to a parable. Your first wife, Haumea, is the first born of all the other women. Think of the time when she was angry with you. She had been sporting with you and then she said in a tired way, 'I want the water.' You asked, 'What water do you want?' She said, 'The water from Poliahu of Mauna Kea.' You took a water-jar and made a hole so that the water always leaked out, and then you went to the pit of Pele. That woman Pele was very old and blear-eyed, so that she could not see you well, and you returned to Haumea. She was that wife of yours. If you escape this mo-o wife she will seek my life. It is my thought to save your life, so that you can look into the eyes of your first wife."

The beautiful dragon-woman had told him to cry with a loud voice when he went back to the cave. But when Puna was going back he went slowly and softly, and saw his wife as a dragon, and understood the words of Hinole. He tried to hide, but was trembling and breathing hard.

His wife heard and quickly changed to a human body, and cursed him, saying: "You are an evil man coming quietly and hiding, but I heard your breath when you thought I would not know you. Perhaps I will eat your eyes. When you were talking with Hinole you learned how to come and see me."

The dragon-goddess was very angry, but Puna did not say anything. She was so angry that the hair on her neck rose up, but it was like a whirlwind, soon quiet and the anger over. They dwelt together, and the woman trusted Puna, and they had peace.

One day Puna was breathing hard, for he was thirsty and wanted the water of the gods.

The woman heard his breathing, and asked, "Why do you breathe like this?" He said: "I want water. We have dwelt together a long time and now I need the water." "What water is this you want?" He said, "I must have the water of Poliahu of Mauna Kea, the snow-covered mountain of Hawaii."

She said, "Why do you want that water?"
He said: "The water of that place is cold and
heavy with ice. In my youth my good grand-
parents always brought water from that place
for me. Wherever I went I carried that water
with me, and when it was gone more would be
brought to me, and so it has been up to the time
that I came to dwell with you. You have water
and I have been drinking it, but it is not the same
as the water mixed with ice, and heavy. But
I would not send you after it, because I know it
is far away and attended with toil unfit for you,
a woman."

The woman bent her head down, then lifted
her eyes, and said: "Your desire for water is not
a hard thing to satisfy. I will go and get the
water."

Before he had spoken of his desire he had
made a little hole in the water-jar, as Hinole had
told him, that the woman might spend a long
time and let him escape.

She arose and went away. He also arose and
followed. He found a canoe and crossed to
Maui. Then he found another boat going to
Hawaii and at last landed at Kau.

He went up and stood on the edge of the pit
of Pele. Those who were living in the crater
saw him, and cried out, "Here is a man, a husband for our sister." He quickly went down

into the crater and dwelt with them. He told all about his journey. Pele heard these words, and said: "Not very long and your wife will be here coming after you, and there will be a great battle, but we will not let you go or you will be killed, because she is very angry against you. She has held you, the husband of our sister Haumea. She should find her own husband and not take what belongs to another. You stay with us and at the right time you can go back to your wife."

Kiha-wahine went to Poliahu, but could not fill the water-jar. She poured the water in and filled the jar, but when the jar was lifted it became light. She looked back and saw the water lying on the ground, and her husband far beyond at the pit of Pele. Then she became angry and called all the dragons of Molokai, Lanai, Maui, Kahoolawe, and Hawaii.

When she had gathered all the dragons she went up to Kilauea and stood on the edge of the crater and called all the people below, telling them to give her the husband. They refused to give Puna up, crying out: "Where is your husband? This is the husband of our sister; he does not belong to you, O mischief-maker."

Then the dragon-goddess said, "If you do not give up this man, of a truth I will send quickly all my people and fill up this crater and capture all your fires." The dragons threw their drooling saliva in the pit, and almost destroyed the fire of the pit where Pele lived, leaving Ka-moho-alii's place untouched.

Then the fire moved and began to rise with great strength, burning off all the saliva of the dragons. Kiha-wahine and the rest of the dragons could not stand the heat even a little while, for the fire caught them and killed a large part of them in that place. They tried to hide in the clefts of the rocks. The earthquakes opened the rocks and some of the dragons hid, but fire followed the earthquakes and the fleeing dragons. Kiha-wahine ran and leaped down the precipice into a fish-pond called by the name of the shadow, or aka, of the dragon, Loko-aka (the shadow lake).

So she was imprisoned in the pond, husbandless, scarcely escaping with her life. When she went back to Molokai she meant to kill Hinole, because she was very angry for his act in aiding Puna to escape. She wanted to punish him, but Hinole saw the trouble coming from his sister, so arose and leaped into the sea, becoming a fish in the ocean.

When he dove into the sea Kiha-wahine went down after him and tried to find him in the small and large coral caves, but could not catch him. He became the Hinalea, a fish dearly loved by the fishermen of the islands. The dragon-goddess continued seeking, swimming swiftly from place to place.

Ounauna saw her passing back and forth, and said, "What are you seeking, O Kiha-wahine?" She said, "I want Hinole." Ounauna said: "Unless you listen to me you cannot get him, just as when you went to Hawaii you could not get your husband from Pele. You go and get the vine inalua and come back and make a basket and put it down in the sea. After a while dive down and you will find that man has come inside. Then catch him."

The woman took the vine, made the basket, came down and put it in the sea. She left it there a little while, then dove down. There was no Hinole in the basket, but she saw him swimming along outside of the basket. She went up, waited awhile, came down again and saw him still swimming outside. This she did again and again, until her eyes were red because she could not catch him. Then she was angry, and went to Ounauna and said: "O slave, I will kill you to-day. Perhaps you told the truth, but I have been deceived, and will chase you until you die."

Ounauna said: "Perhaps we should talk before I die. I want you to tell me just what you have done, then I will know whether you followed directions. Tell me in a few words. Perhaps I forgot something."

The dragon said, "I am tired of your words and I will kill you." Then Ounauna said, "Suppose I die, what will you do to correct any mistakes you have made?"

Then she told how she had taken vines and made a basket and used it. Ounauna said: "I forgot to tell you that you must get some sea eggs and crabs, pound and mix them together and put them inside the basket. Put the mouth of the basket down. Leave it for a little while, then dive down and find your brother inside. He will not come out, and you can catch him." This is the way the Hinalea is caught to this day.

After she had caught her brother she took him to the shore to kill him, but he persuaded her to set him free. This she did, compelling him ever after to retain the form of the fish Hinalea.

Kiha-wahine then went to the island Maui and dwelt in a deep pool near the old royal town of Lahaina.

After Pele had her battle with the dragons, and Puna had escaped according to the directions of Hinole, he returned to Oahu and saw his wife, Haumea, a woman with many names, as if she were the embodiment of many goddesses.

After Puna disappeared, Kou became the new

chief of Oahu. Puna went to live in the mountains above Kalihi-uka. One day Haumea went out fishing for crabs at Heeia, below the precipice of Koolau, where she was accustomed to go. Puna came to a banana plantation, ate, and lay down to rest. He fell fast asleep and the watchmen of the new chief found him. They took his loin-cloth, and tied his hands behind his back, bringing him thus to Kou, who killed him and hung the body in the branches of a breadfruit-tree. It is said that this was at Wai-kaha-lulu just below the steep diving rocks of the Nuuanu stream.

When Haumea returned from gathering moss and fish to her home in Kalihi-uka, she heard of the death of her husband. She had taken an akala vine, made a pa-u, or skirt, of it, and tied it around her when she went fishing, but she forgot all about it, and as she hurried down to see the body of her husband, all the people turned to look at her, and shouted out, "This is the wife of the dead man."

She found Puna hanging on the branches. Then she made that breadfruit-tree open. Leaving her pa-u on the ground where she stood, she stepped inside the tree and bade it close about her and appear the same as before. The akala, of which the pa-u had been made, lay where it was left, took root and grew into a large vine.

The fat of the body of Puna fell down through the branches and the dogs ate below the tree. One of these dogs belonged to the chief Kou. It came back to the house, played with the chief, then leaped, caught him by the throat and killed him.

NOTE.—This is the same legend as "The Wonderful Breadfruit Tree" published in the "Legends of Old Honolulu," but the names are changed and the time is altered from the earliest days of Hawaiian lore to the almost historic period of King Kakuhihewa, whose under-chief mentioned in this legend gave the name to Old Honolulu, as for centuries it bore the name "Kou." The legend is new, however, in so far as it gives the account of the infatuation of Puna for Kiha-wahine, the dragon-goddess, and his final escape from her.

BREAD   FRUIT.

XVII

KE-AU-NINI

KU–AHA–ILO was a demon who had no parents. His great effort was to find something to eat—men or any other kind of food. He was a kupua—one who was sometimes an animal and sometimes a man. He was said to be the father of Pele, the goddess of volcanic fires.

Nakula-uka and Nakula-kai were the parents of Hiilei, who was the mother of Ke-au-nini. Nakula-kai told her husband that she was with child. He told her that he was glad, and if it were a boy he would name him, but if a girl she should name the child.

The husband went out fishing, and Nakula-kai went to see her parents, Kahuli and Kakela. The hot sun was rising, so she put leaves over her head and came to the house. Her father was asleep. She told her mother about her condition. Kahuli awoke and turning over shook the land by his motion, *i.e.*, the far-away divine land of Nuu-mea-lani. He asked his daughter why she had come, and when she told him he studied the signs and foretold the birth of a girl who should be named Hina.

Kahuli's wife questioned his knowledge. He said: "I will prepare awa in a cup, cover it with white kapa, and chant a prayer. I will lift the cover, and if the awa is still there I am at fault. If the awa has disappeared I am correct. It will be proved by the awa disappearing that a girl will be born.

"I was up above Niihau.
O Ku! O Kane! O Lono!
I have dug a hole,
Planted the bamboo;
The bamboo has grown;
Find that bamboo!
It has grown old.
The green-barked bamboo has a green bark;
The white-barked bamboo has a white bark.
Fragments of rain are stinging the skin—
Rain fell that day in storms,
Water pouring in streams.
Mohoalii is by the island,
Island cut off at birth from the mainland;
Many islands as children were born."

A girl was born, and the grandparents kept the child, calling her Hina. She cried, and the grandmother took her in her arms and sang:

"Fishing, fishing, your father is fishing,
Catching the opoa-pea."

Nakula-kai went down to her home. Her husband returned from fishing. He said he thought another child was born. He had heard the thunder, but no storm. She told him that a boy was born. Nakula-uka named that boy Ke-au-miki (stormy or choppy current). Ten days afterward another boy was born. He was named Ke-au-kai (current toward the beach).

These children had no food but awa. Their hair was not cut. They were taken inside a tabu temple and brought up. Nakula-uka and his wife after a long time had another girl named Hiilei (lifted like a lei on the head). The grand-parents took the child. She was very beautiful and was kept tabu. Her husband should be either a king or a male kupua of very high birth. When she had grown up she heard noises below her woodland home several times, and she was very curious. She was told, "That comes from the surf-riding."

Hiilei wanted to go down and see. The grandmother said, "Do not go, for it would mean your death." Once more came the noise, and she was told it was "spear-throwing." The girl wanted to know how that was done. The grand-parents warned her that there was great danger, saying: "The path is full of trouble. Dragons lie beside the way. Ku-aha-ilo, the mo-o [dragon], is travelling through the sky, the clouds, the earth, and the forest. His tongue is thrusting every way to find food. He is almost starved, and now plans to assume his human form and come to Nuu-mea-lani, seeking to find some one for food. You should not go down to the beach of Honua-lewa [the field of sports]."

But Hiilei was very persistent, so the grandmother at last gave permission, saying: "I will let you go, but here are my commands. You are quite determined to go down, but listen to me. Ku-aha-ilo is very hungry, and is seeking food these days. When you go down to the grove of kukui-trees, there Ku-aha-ilo will await you and you will be afraid that he will catch you. Do not be afraid. Pass that place bravely. Go on the lower side—the valley-side—and you cannot be touched. When that one sees you he will change into his god-body and stand as a mo-o. Do not show that you are afraid. He cannot touch you unless you are afraid and flee. Keep your fear inside and give 'Aloha' and say, 'You are a strangely beautiful one.' The dragon will think you are not afraid. Then that mo-o will take another body. He will become a great caterpillar. Caterpillars will surround you. You must give 'Aloha' and praise. Thus you must do with all the mysterious bodies of Ku-aha-ilo without showing any fear. Then Ku-aha-ilo will become a man and will be your husband."

So the girl went down, dressed gorgeously by the grandmother in a skirt of rainbow colors, flowers of abundant perfumes—nothing about her at fault.

She came to the kukui grove and looked all around, seeing nothing, but passing further along she saw a mist rising. A strong wind was coming. The sun was hot in the sky, making her cheeks red like lehua flowers. She went up some high places looking down on the sea. Then she heard footsteps behind her. She looked back and saw a strange body following. She became afraid and trembled, but she remembered the words of her grandmother, and turned and said, "Aloha," and the strange thing went away. She went on and again heard a noise and looked back. A whirlwind was coming swiftly after her. Then there was thunder and lightning.

Hiilei said: "Aloha. Why do you try to make me afraid? Come in your right body, for I know that you are a real man."

Everything passed away. She went on again, but after a few steps she felt an earthquake. Afraid, she sat down. She saw a great thing rising like a cloud twisting and shutting out the sun, moving and writhing—a great white piece of earth in front of a whirlwind.

She was terribly frightened and fell flat on the ground as if dead. Then she heard the spirit of her grandmother calling to her to send away her fear, saying: "This is the one of whom I told you. Don't be afraid." She looked at the cloud, and the white thing became omaomao (green). Resolutely she stood up, shook her rainbow skirt and flowers. The perfumes were scattered in the air and she started on. Then the dragons, a multitude, surrounded her, climbing upon her to throw her down. Her skin was creeping, but she remembered her grandmother and said: "Alas, O most beautiful ones, this is the first time I have ever seen you. If my grandmother were here we would take you back to our home and entertain you, and you should be my playmates. But I cannot return, so I must say 'Farewell.'"

Then the dragons disappeared and the caterpillars came into view after she had gone on a little way. The caterpillars' eyes were protruding as they rose up and came against her, but she said, "Aloha."

Then she saw another form of Ku-aha-ilo—a stream of blood flowing like running water. She was more frightened than at any other time, and cried to her grandfather: "E Kahuli, I am afraid! Save my life, O my grandfather!" He did not know she had gone down. He told his wife that he saw Ku-aha-ilo surrounding someone on the path. He went into his temple and prayed:

> "Born is the night,
> Born is the morning,
> Born is the thunder,
> Born is the lightning,
> Born is the heavy rain,
> Born is the rain which calls us;
> The clouds of the sky gather."

Then Kahuli twisted his kapa clothes full of lightning and threw them into the sky. A fierce and heavy rain began to fall. Streams of water rushed toward the place where Hiilei stood fighting with that stream of blood in which the dragon was floating. The blood was all washed away and the dragon became powerless.

Ku-aha-ilo saw that he had failed in all these attempts to terrify Hiilei. His eyes flashed and he opened his mouth. His tongue was thrusting viciously from side to side. His red mouth was like the pit of Pele. His teeth were gnashing, his tail lashing.

Hiilei stood almost paralyzed by fear, but remembered her grandmother. She felt that death was near when she faced this awful body of Ku-aha-ilo. But she hid her fear and called a welcome to this dragon. Then the dragon fell into pieces, which all became nothing. The fragments flew in all directions.

While Hiilei was watching this, all the evil disappeared and a handsome man stood before her. Hiilei asked him gently, "Who are you, and from what place do you come?" He said, "I am a man of this place." "No," said Hiilei, "you are not of this land. My grandparents and I are the only ones. This is our land. From what place do you come?" He replied: "I am truly from the land above the earth, and I have

come to find a wife for myself.   Perhaps you will
be my wife."   She said that she did not want a
husband at that time.   She wanted to go down
to the sea.

He persuaded her to marry him and then go
down and tell her brothers that she had married
Ku-aha-ilo.   If a boy was born he must be called
Ke-au-nini-ula-o-ka-lani (The red, restful current
of the heavens).   This would be their only child.
He gave her signs for the boy, saying, "When
the boy says to you, 'Where is my father?' you
can tell him, 'Here is the stick or club Kaaona
and this malo or girdle Ku-ke-anuenue.'   He
must take these things and start out to find me."
He slowly disappeared, leaving Hiilei alone.   She
went down to the sea.   The people saw her
coming, a very beautiful woman, and they
shouted a glad welcome.

She went out surf-riding, sported awhile, and
then her grandfather came and took her home.
After a time came the signs of the birth of a chief.
Her son was born and named Ke-au-nini.   This
was in the land Kuai-he-lani.   Kahuli almost
turned over.   The land was shaken and tossed.
This was one of the divine lands from which the
ancestors of the Hawaiians came.   Pii-moi, a
god of the sun, asked Akoa-koa, the coral, "What
is the matter with the land?"   Akoa-koa replied,
"There is a kupua—a being with divine powers—

being born, with the gifts of Ku-aha-ilo." Pii-
moi was said to be below Papaku-lolo, taking care
of the foundation of the earth. The brothers
were in their temple. Ke-au-kai heard the signs
in the leaves and knew that his sister had a child,
and proposed to his brother to go over and get
the child. The mother had left it on a pile of
sugar-cane leaves. They met their sister and
asked for the child. Then they took it, wrapped
it in a soft kapa and went back to the temple.
The temple drum sounded as they came in,
beaten by invisible hands.

The boy grew up. The mother after a time
wanted to see the child, and went to the temple.
She had to wait a little, then the boy came out
and said he would soon come to her. She rejoiced to see such a beautiful boy as her Ke-au-
nini-ula-o-ka-lani. They talked and rejoiced in
their mutual affection. An uncle came and sent
her away for a time. The boy returned to the
temple, and his uncle told him he could soon go
to be with his mother. Then came an evil night
and the beating of the spirit drum. A mist
covered the land. There was wailing among the
menehunes (fairy folk). Ke-au-nini went away
covered by the mist, and no one saw him go.

He came to his grandfather's house, saw an
old man sleeping and a war-club by the door. He
took this club and lifted it to strike the old man,

but the old man caught the club. The boy dropped it and tried to catch the old man. The old man held him and asked who he was and to what family he belonged. The boy said: "I belong to Kahuli and Kakela, to Nakula-uka and Nakula-kai. I am the son of Ku-aha-ilo and Hiilei. I have been brought up by Ke-au-miki and Ke-au-kai. I seek my mother."

The old man arose, took his drum and beat it. Hiilei and her mother came out to meet the boy. They put sacrifices in their temple for him and chanted to their ancestor-gods:

> "O Keke-hoa-lani, dwell here;
> Here are wind and rain."

By and by Ke-au-nini asked his mother, "Where is my father?" She told him: "You have no father in the lands of the earth. He belongs to the atmosphere above. You cannot go to find him. He never told me the path-way to his home. You had better stay with me." He replied: "No I cannot stay here. I must go to find my father." He was very earnest in his purpose.

His mother said: "If you make a mistake, your father will kill you and then eat you and take all your lands. He will destroy the forests and the food plants, and all will be devoured by your father. His kingdom is tabu. If you go, take great care of the gifts, for with these things you succeed, but without them you die." She showed him the war-club and the rainbow-girdle, and gave them into his care. The boy took the gifts, kissed his mother, went outside and looked up into the sky.

He saw wonderful things. A long object passed before him, part of which was on the earth, but the top was lost in the clouds. This was Niu-loa-hiki, one of the ancestor-gods of the night. This was a very tall cocoanut-tree, from which the bark of coconuts fell in the shape of boats. He took one of these boats in his hands, saying, "How can I ride in this small canoe?"

He went down to the sea, put the bark boat in the water, got in and sailed away until the land of Nuu-mea-lani was lost. His uncle, Ke-au-kai, saw him going away, and prayed to the aumakuas (ancestral ghost-gods) to guard the boy. The boy heard the soft voice of the far-off surf, and as he listened he saw a girl floating in the surf. He turned his boat and joined her. She told him to go back, or he would be killed. She was Moho-nana, the first-born child of Ku-aha-ilo.

When she learned that this was her half-brother, she told him that her father was sleeping. If he awoke, the boy would be killed.

The boy went to the shore of this strange land. Ku-aha-ilo saw him coming, and breathed out the wind of his home against the boy. It was like a black whirlwind rushing to the sea.

The boy went on toward his father's tabu place, up to Kalewa, in the face of the storm. He saw the tail of Ku-aha-ilo sweep around against him to kill him. He began his chants and incantations and struck his war-club on the ground. Lava came out and fire was burning all around him. He could not strike the tail, nor could the tail strike him. Ku-aha-ilo sent many other enemies, but the war-club turned them aside. The earth was shaking, almost turning upside down as it was struck by the war-club. Great openings let lava fires out. Ku-aha-ilo came out of his cave to fight. His mouth was open, his tongue outstretching, his eyes glaring, but the boy was not afraid. He took his club, whirled it in his hand, thinking his father would see it, but his father did not see it. The boy leaped almost inside the mouth and struck with the club up and down, every stroke making an opening for fire.

The father tried to shut his mouth, but the boy leaped to one side and struck the father's head. The blow glanced aside and made a great hole in the earth, which let out fire. The dragon body disappeared and came back in another form, as a torrent of blood. Ke-au-nini thrust it aside. Then a handsome man stood before him with wild eyes, demanding who he was. Ku-aha-ilo had forgotten his son, and the miraculous war-club which he had given to Hiilei, so he began to fight with his hands. Ke-au-nini laid his club down. The father was near the end of his strength, and said, "Let our anger cease, that we may know each other." The boy was very angry and said: "You have treated me cruelly, when I only came to see you and to love you. You would have taken my young life for sacrifice. Now you tell me you belong to the temple of my ancestors in Nuu-mea-lani." Then he caught his father and lifted him up. He tossed him, dizzy and worn out, into the air, and catching the body broke it over his knee. Ku-aha-ilo had killed and eaten all his people, so that no one was left in his land. The boy's sister saw the battle and went away to Ka-lewa-lani (the divine far-away cloud-land).

Ke-au-nini returned on his ocean journey to Nuu-mea-lani. The uncle saw a mist covering the sea and saw the sign of a chief in it, and knew that the boy was not dead, but had killed Ku-aha-ilo. The boy came and greeted them and told the story. He remained some time in the temple and dreamed of a beautiful woman.

The brothers talked about the power of Ke-au-nini who had killed his father, a man without parents, part god and part man. They thought

he would now kill them.   Ke-au-nini became pale
and thin and sick, desiring the woman of his
dream.   Finally he told the brothers to find that
woman or he would kill them.

Ke-au-kai told him that he would consult the
gods.   Then he made a red boat with a red mast
and a red sail and told Ke-au-miki to go after
Hiilei, their sister.

Hiilei came down to stay with her son while
the brothers went away to find the girl.   Ke-au-
kai (Broad sea-current) said to Ke-au-miki
(Chopped-up current): "You sit in front, I behind.   Let this be our law.   You must not turn
back to look at me.   You must not speak to me.
I must not speak to you, or watch you."

Ke-au-miki went to his place in the boat.   The
other stood with one foot in the boat and one on
the land.   He told the boy they would go.   If
they found a proper girl they would return; if
not, they would not come back.   They pushed
the boat far out to sea by one paddle-stroke.
Another stroke and land was out of sight.
Swiftly leaped the boat over the ocean.

They saw birds on the island Kaula.   One
bird flew up.   Heavy winds almost upset the
boat and filled it with water up to their chins.
They caught the paddles, bailing-cups, and loose
boards for seats, and held them safe.

The wind increased like a cyclone over them.

Thus in the storm they floated on the sea. Ke-au-nini by his sorcery saw the swamped canoe. He ran and told his mother. She sent him to the temple to utter incantations:

"O wind, wini-wini [sharp-pointed];
O wind full of stinging points;
O wind rising at Vavau,
At Hii-ka-lani;
Stamped upon, trodden upon by the wind.
Niihau is the island;
Ka-pali-kala-hale is the chief."

This chant of Ke-au-nini reached Ke-au-kai, and the wind laid aside its anger. Its strength was made captive and the sea became calm.

The boat came to the surface, and they bailed it out and took their places. Ke-au-kai said to his brother: "What a wonderful one is that boy of ours! We must go to Niihau." They saw birds, met a boat and fisherman, and found Niihau. When the Niihau people saw them coming on a wonderful surf wave, they shouted about the arrival of the strangers. The chief Ka-pali-kala-hale came down as the surf swept the boat inland. He took the visitors to his house and gave gifts of food, kapas, and many other things. Then they went on their way. When they were between Niihau and Kauai, the wind drove the boat back. A whirlwind threw water into the boat, swamping it. It was sinking and all the goods were floating away.

Ke-au-nini again saw the signs of trouble and chanted:

> "The wind of Kauai comes; it touches; it strikes;
> Rising, whirling; boat filled with water;
> The boat slipping down in the sea;
> The outrigger sticks in the sand.
> Kauai is the island;
> Ka-pali-o-ka-la-lau is chief."

The sea became calm. The boat was righted and the floating goods were put in. They met canoes and went on a mighty surf wave up the sands of the beach.

The people shouted, "Aloha!" The chiefess of that part of Kauai was surf-riding and heard the people shouting welcome, so she came to land and found the visitors sitting on the sand, resting. She took them to the royal home. All the people of Kauai came together to meet the strangers, making many presents.

The brothers found no maids sufficiently perfect, so they crossed over to Oahu, meeting other trials. At last they went to Hawaii to the place where Haina-kolo lived, a chiefess and a kua (goddess).

This was above Kawaihae. They went to Kohala, seeking the dream-land of Ke-au-nini, and then around to Waipio Valley. There they saw a rainbow resting over the home of a tabu chief, Ka-lua-hine. They landed near the door of the Under-world. This entrance is through a cave under water. There they saw the shadow of Milu, the ruler of the dead. Milu's people called out, "Here are men breaking the tabu of the chief." Olopana, a very high chief, heard the shouts while he was in the temple in the valley. He saw the visitors chased by the people, running here and there. Haina-kolo, his sister, was tabu. Watchmen were on the outside of her house. They also saw the two men and the people pursuing, and told Haina-kolo, and she ordered one of the watchmen to go out and say to the strangers, "Oh, run swiftly; run, run, and come inside this temple!" They heard and ran in. The people stopped on the outside of the wall around the house. This was a tabu drum place, and not a temple of safety.

Olopana was in the heiau (temple) Pakaa-lana. Haina-kolo asked who they were. They said they were from Hawaii. She said, "No, you have come from the sea." Hoo-lei-palaoa, one of her watchmen, called, and men came and caught the two strangers, taking them to Olo-pana, who was very angry because they had come into the temple of his sister. So he ordered his men to take them at once and carry them to a prison house to die on the morrow. He said if the prisoners escaped, the watchmen should die and their bodies be burned in the fire. Toward morning the two prisoners talked together and uttered incantations. Ke-au-nini saw by the signs that they were in some trouble and chanted in the ears of the watchmen: "They shall not die. They shall not die."

The watchmen reported to Olopana what they had heard, then returned to watch. The moon was rising and the two prisoners were talking. Ke-au-kai told his brother to look at the moon, saying: "This means life. The cloud passes, morning comes." Ka-au-kai prayed and chanted. The watchmen again reported to Olopana, giving the words of the chant. In this chant the family names were given. Olopana said: "These are the names of my mother's people. My mother is Hina. Her sister is Hiilei. Her brothers are Ke-au-kai and Ke-au-miki. They were all living at Kuai-he-lani. Hina and her husband Ku went away to Waipio. There she had her child, Haina-kolo."

Olopana sent messengers for Hina, who was like the rising moon, giving life, and for her husband Ku, who was at Napoopoo, asking them to come and look at these prisoners. They ran swiftly and arrived by daylight. Hina had been troubled all night. Messengers called: "Awake! Listen to the chant of the prisoners, captured yesterday." And they reported the prayers of Ke-au-kai. Hina arose and went to the heiau (temple) and heard the story of her brothers,

who came also with the warriors. Olopana
heard Hina wailing with her brothers, and was
afraid that his mother would kill him because
he had treated his visitors so badly. The
strangers told her they had come to find a wife
for Ke-au-nini. They had looked at the beautiful
women of all the islands and had found none
except the woman at Waipio. Then they told
about the anger of the people, the pursuit, and
their entrance into the tabu temple.

Hina commanded Olopana to come before
them. He took warriors and chiefs and came
over to the temple and stood before his parents.
Hina pronounced judgment, saying: "This chief
shall live because he sent for me. The chiefs and
people who pursued shall die and be cooked in
the oven in which they thought to place the
strangers."

Ku's warriors captured Olopana's men and
took them away prisoners, but Olopana was
spared and made welcome by his uncle. And
they all feasted together for days. Then the
brothers prepared to go after Ke-au-nini.

One man who heard the wailing of the brothers
and knew of the coming of Hina went to his
house, took his wife and children and ran by way
of Hilo to Puna-luu. It was said this man took
his calabash to get water at the spring Kauwila,
and an owl picked a hole in it and let the water

out. For this the owl was injured by a stone which was thrown at him, and he told the other birds. They said he was rightly punished for his fault.

The brothers found their red boat, launched it, and bade farewell to the chief's people and lands. They returned to Kuai-he-lani, like a flash of lightning speeding along the coast from south to west. The boy in the temple saw them in their swift boat. He told Hiilei and prepared for their coming. They landed, feasted, and told their story. Then they prepared for their journey to Waipio. Their boat was pulled by fish in place of boatmen, and these disappeared upon arrival at Hawaii. Ke-au-kai went first to meet Olopana, who ran down to see Ke-au-nini and asked how he came. Ke-au-nini said, "There was no wandering, no murmuring, no hunger, no pinched faces."

Then they feasted while over them thunder and lightning played and mist covered the house. Awa was thrown before the spirit of the thunder and they established tabus.

Olopana had trouble with his priests and became angry and wanted to punish them because they did not know how to do their work so well as Ke-au-nini. They could make thunder and lightnings and earthquakes, but Ke-au-nini blew toward the east and something like a man appeared in a cloud of dust; he put his right hand in the dust and began to make land. Olopana saw this and thought it was done by the kahunas (priests) and so he forgave them, thinking they had more power than Ke-au-nini. Later he ordered them to be killed and cooked. Olopana asked Ke-au-nini, "Which of the tabu houses do you wish to take as your residence?" Ke-au-nini replied: "My house is the lightning, the bloody sky, or the dark cloud hanging over Kuai-he-lani, down the ridge or extending cape Ke-au-oku, where Ku of Kauhika is, where multitudes of eyes bend low before the gods. The house of my parents—there is where I dwell. You have heard of that place."

Olopana was greatly astonished, bowed his head and thought for a long time, then said: "We will set apart our tabu days for worship, and I will see your tabu place—you in your place and I outside. When you are through your days of tabu you must return and we will live together."

Ke-au-nini raised his eyes and spoke softly to the clouds above him: "O my parents, this my brother-in-law wishes to see our dwelling-place, therefore call Ke-au-kai to send down our tabu dwelling-place."

Ke-au-kai was near him, and said: "We had very many troubles on the ocean in coming after the one whom you want for your wife. You aided us to escape; perhaps the old man in the skies will hear you if you call." Then Ke-au-nini turned toward the east:

> "Ke-au-nini has his home,
> His home with his mother.
> Hiilei, the wife,
> She was the child of Nakula-uka,
> The first-born Kakela.
> The cheeks grow red;
> And the eyes flash fire.
> In the Lewa-lani [heavens],
> The very heart of the lightning.
> A double rainbow is high arched.
> The voice of the Kana-mu are heard.
> Calling and crying are the Kana-wa.
> [The Kana-mu and the Kana-wa were companies of little
>   people, *i.e.*, fairies.]
> I continually call to you, O little ones,
> Come here with the white feathers,
> Let feathers come here together;
> Let all the colors of the tortoise-back
> Gather and descend;
> Let all the posts stand strong;
> Braced shall be the house;
> Fasten in also the smoke-colored feathers;
> Work swiftly and complete our tabu house."

Then the darkness of evening came, and in the shadows the little people labored in the moonless night. Soon their work was done, the house finished, and a sacred drum placed inside. When the clear sky of the morning rested over, and the sun made visible the fairy home in the early dawn, the people cried out with wonder at the beautiful thing before them. There stood a house of glowing feathers of all colors. Posts

and rafters of polished bones shone like the ivory
teeth of the whale, tinted in the smoke of a fire.
Softly swayed the feathered thatch in a gentle
breeze, rustling through the surrounding coco-
trees. Most beautiful it was, as in the chant of
Lilinoe:

> "Hulei Lilinoe me Kuka-hua-ula;
> Hele Hoaheo i kai o Mokuleia."

> "Lifted up, blown by the wind are
> The falls down to the sea of Mokuleia."

Ke-au-nini told his brother-in-law, "Oh, my
brother, look upon my tabu dwelling-place as
you wished."

Olopana was very curious, and asked, "How
many people are needed to make a house like
this so quickly?" Ke-au-nini laughed and said,
"You have seen my people: there are three of
us who built this house—I, the chief, and my
two friends."

He did not give the names of the little people,
Kana-mu and Kana-wa, who were really great
multitudes, like the menehunes who made the
ditch at Waimea, Kauai. They were the one-
night people. All this work was finished while
they alone could see clearly to use their magic
powers.

Inside the house lay soft mats made from feathers of many birds, and sleeping-couches better
than had ever been seen before. Ke-au-nini
said to his brother-in-law: "We are now ready

to have the tabu of our house. My parents will enter with me."

Olopana asked his kahunas if it were right for the parents to stay with the chief during a tabu, under the law of their land. The priests consulted and told Olopana that this was all right. They had no power to forbid. The parents had divine power, so also the boy, both alike, and could dwell together without breaking tabu. Then they said, "If you forbid, you will be landless."

Ke-au-kai and Ke-au-miki entered the house with their young chief. Ke-au-miki beat the sacred drum, announcing the tabu. They poured and drank awa, ate sugar-cane and chanted softly to the rhythm of the drum. Olopana was filled with jealousy because all was hidden from him. He did not know what a drum was. He had only known a time of tabu, but not the secret drum, and the soft chant.

During the ten days' tabu Ke-au-nini did not see his wife, but remained shut in his place. Olopana called for all the people to bring presents. When the tabu was over and the temple door opened, Ke-au-nini and Haina-kolo prepared for the marriage.

All the people came bringing feather mats, food, fish, and awa, which had been growing on a tree. Hamakua sent food and fish; Hilo sent olona and feathers; Puna sent mats and awa from the trees; Kau sent kapa; Kona sent red kapas; Kohala sent its wonderful noted sweet potatoes. The young chiefess appeared before all the people, coming from her tabu place, and she saw all the fine presents, and a great coconut-leaf lanai (porch) prepared by her brother. She came there before her parents and brother. They were waiting for Ke-au-nini, who delayed coming. Olopana asked his priests: "Why does the young chief fail to appear? We are all ready for the marriage feast." The priest said to Olopana: "Do you think that you can treat this man as one of us? He is a god on his father's side and also on his mother's. He is very high. It is on his mother's side that you are related. You should go to him with a sacrifice. Take a black pig, a cup of awa, a black chicken, and a coco-nut. If we do not do these things we shall not know where he is staying, for he is under the care of the gods. Now is the right time to go with the offering. Go quickly. The sun is rising high in the sky."

Olopana quickly gathered the offerings and went away to sacrifice before Ke-au-nini. He called him thus:

> "Rise up! Let your strength look inland;
> Let your might look toward the sea;
> Let your face look upward;
> Look up to the sun over your head;

The strange night has passed.   Awake!
Here are the offerings,—
Food for the gods:
Let life come!"

He set the pig free and it ran to the feet of
Ke-au-nini.   The chicken did the same, and the
other offerings were laid before the door.   Olopana went back.   Ke-au-nini and his uncles
awoke.   He said to them: "Now the tabu is
lifted.   Now the hour of the marriage has come.
We must prepare to go down to the sea.   We
shall see the sports of this land.   Soon we shall
meet the priests and the people."

They arose and opened their bundles of kapa,
very fine and soft for red malos (girdles) for the
uncles.   Ke-au-nini put on his malo, called
Ke-kea-awe-awe-ula (the red girdle with long
ends, shaded in the tints of the rainbow) and
his red feather cloak and his red feather helmet,
nodding like a bird.   His skin, polished and
perfumed, shone resplendently.   He was most
gorgeous in his appearance.

When he went out of his house, thatched with
bird feathers and built of polished bones, darkness spread over the sky.   The voices of the
little fairies, the Kana-mu and Kana-wa were
heard.   The people in the great coconut lanai
were filled with wonder, for they had never seen
darkness come in this way.   It was like the sun
eclipsed.   When Ke-au-nini and his companions

entered the lanai, the darkness passed away and
all the people saw them in their splendor. The
chiefs opened a way for the three. Ke-au-miki
came in first and the people thought he was the
husband, but when Ke-au-kai came they said,
"This one is more beautiful," and when Ke-au-
nini passed before them they fell on their faces,
although he had a gauze kapa thrown over him.
He passed on between rows of chiefs to the
place of marriage. His uncles stepped aside, and
then he threw off his thin kapa and the people
shouted again and again until the echoes shook
the precipices around the valley.

Then Haina-kolo came out of her house near
by and was guided to the side of her husband.
As she saw him her heart melted and flowed to
him like the mingling of floating sea-mosses.
Olopana arose and said: "O chiefs and people,
I have been asked to come here to the marriage
of my sister with one whom she has met in dreams
and loved. I agree to this wedding. Our parents approve, and the gods have given their signs.
Our chiefess shall belong to the stranger. You
shall obey him. I will do as he may direct.
They shall now become husband and wife."

The people shouted again and again, saying,
"This is the husband of our chiefess." Then
began the hookupu. Six districts brought six
piles of offerings. There were treasures and

treasures of all kinds. Then came the wonderful feast of all the people.

The fish companions of Ke-au-nini, who had drawn his boat from Kuai-he-lani, wanted Haina-kolo for themselves. While they were at the feast they found they could not get her, and they grew cold and ashamed and angry. Soon they broke away from the feast. Moi and Uhu ran away to the sea and returned to their homes. Niu-loa-hiki (a great eel) looked at Ke-au-nini and said: "You are very strange. I thought I should have my reward this day, but the winning has come to you. I am angry, because you are my servant. It is a shame for the chiefs of Hawaii to let you become their ruler." His angry eyes flashed fire, he opened his mouth and started to cry out again, but the people saw him and shouted: "Look, look, there is an eel that comes to the land. He runs and dives into the sea. This eel, Niu-loa-hiki, is more evil than any other of all the family of eels."

Then all the fish ran off angry at this failure and gathered in the sea for consultation. Uhu said he would return at once to Makapuu. He was the Uhu who had the great battle with Kawelo when he was caught in a net. Moi went to the rough water outside the harbor. Kumu-nuiaiake went to Hilo. He was the huge fish with which Limaloa had a great battle when he came to visit Hawaii. He was killed by Limaloa. Hou and Awela went wherever they could find a ditch to swim in.

The people feasted on the mullet of Lolakea and the baked dogs of Hilo and the humpbacked mullet of Waiakea and all the sweet things of Hawaii. Then the sports commenced and there was surf-riding, dancing, wrestling, and boxing.

Kawelo-hea, the surf-rider of Kawa in Oahu, was the best surf-rider. Hina-kahua, the child of the battling-places of Kohala, was the best boxer. Pilau-hulu, the noted boy of Olaa, was the best puhenehene-player. Lilinoe was the best konane-player. Luu-kia was the best kilu-player. She was a relative of Haina-kolo.

When the sports were over they returned to the chief's house and slept. Haina-kolo was one who did not closely adhere to the tabu. She ate the tabu things, which were sacred, belonging to the gods, such as bananas and luau. Ke-au-nini had always carefully, from his birth to marriage-day, observed the tabu, but, following the example of his wife, soon laid aside his carefulness, and lived in full disregard of all restraint for a time.

Then Ke-au-nini left Haina-kolo and returned to Kuai-he-lani because dissensions arose between them on account of their wrong-doing.

He did not tell his wife or friends, or even his uncles, but he took his coconut-boat to go back to his home secretly. When he was far out in the ocean his sister saw him from her home in Lewa-lani (the blue sky). She sent Kana-ula, her watchman, to go out and guard him and bring him to her. Kana-ula was a strong wind blowing with the black clouds which rise before a storm.

In a little while the watchman saw Ke-au-nini off Kohala, and by his great strength lifted Ke-au-nini and placed him on Kuai-he-lani, where he saw his mother and relatives. Then he went up to Lewa-lani to his sister and dwelt with her to forget his love for Haina-kolo.

Haina-kolo had a great love for her husband, never making any trouble before they separated. Her love for him was burning and full of passion, while she grieved over his disappearance. She soon had a child. The priests living in the heiau (temple), Pakaalana, beat their drums, and all Waipio knew that a chief was born.

Haina-kolo began to go about like one crazed, longing to see the eyes of her husband. She took her child and launched out in the ocean. The boat in which she placed the child was the long husk of a coconut. She held fast to this and swam and floated by its side. When they had gone far out in the sea a great wind swept over them and upon them, driving them far out of sight of all land. She looked only for death. This wind was Kana-ula, and had been sent by

Moho, who was very angry at the girl for violating the tabu of the gods and eating the things set apart for the gods. This wind was to blow her far away on the ocean until death came.

When Haina-kolo had been blown a little way she prayed and moved her feet, turning toward the place where she had rejoiced with her husband. Then she offered another prayer and began to swim, but was driven out of sight of land. The wind ceased, its anger passed away, and a new land appeared. She swam toward this new land. Lei-makani, the child, saw this land, which was the high place of Ke-ao-lewa, and chanted:

> "Destroy the first kou * grove;
> Destroy the second kou grove;
> Open a wonderful door in the evening;
> Offer your worship.
> Return, return, O bird!"

The mother said: "No, my child, that is not a bird. Oh, my child, that is Ke-ao-lewa, the land where we shall find a shore."

But she went on patiently, swimming by the capes of Kohala, and came near to the places of noted surf and was almost on the land. Moho saw her still swimming and sent another wind-servant, Makani-kona, the south wind, to drive her again out in the ocean. This south wind came like a whirlwind, sweeping and twisting

* Cordia subcordata.

over the waves, sending Haina-kolo far out in the tossing sea. He thought he had killed her, so he went back to Moho.

Moho asked him about his journey over the seas. He replied, "You sent me to kill, and that I did." She was satisfied and ceased her vigilance. Tired and suffering, Haina-kolo and her child floated far out in the ocean, too weary to swim. Then Lei-makani saw Ke-ao-lewa again lifted up and spread out like the wings of a floating bird. Help came to her in a great shark, Kau-naha-ili-pakapaka (Kau-naha, with a rough skin), belonging to the family of Pii-moi, one of the relatives of Ku, who swam up to her and carried her and the child until he was tired. Haina-kolo was rested and warmed by the sun. She saw that her shark friend was growing weak, so she called to the sun, "O sun, go on your way to the land of Ka-lewa-nuu, and tell Ke-au-nini that we are here at the cape of Ka-ia."

The sun did not hear the cry from the sea. She called again, using the same words. The sun heard this call of Haina-kolo and went on to the place where Ke-au-nini was staying and called to him, "O Ke-au-nini, your wife is near the cape of Ka-ia."

Moho heard the call. She was playing konane with her brother. She made a noise to confuse the words of the sun, and said to her brother,

"O ke ku kela, o ka holo keia. Niole ka luna, kopala ka ele, na ke kea ka ai." "Take this one up. Let that one move. Take that up slowly. The black is blotted out, the white wins."

Then the sun called again, saying the same words, and Ke-au-nini heard, leaped up and left his sister, and went down to Kuai-he-lani and entered the temple, where he was accustomed to sleep, and fell as one dead. While he was reclining, his spirit left his body and went down to Milu and stayed there a long time.

Haina-kolo was very near the land in the afternoon. Soon they came to the beach. There she dug a little hole for her child and laid him in his little boat in it and went up the path like a crazy person to the top of the high precipices of Ka-hula-anu (the cold dancing) and began to eat fruit growing on the trees. She clothed herself in leaves, then rushed into the forest.

Lei-makani was still floating where his mother had left him, near a place where the servants of Luu-kia went fishing every morning to get the food loved by the chiefs. Two men, Ka-holo-holo-uka and Ka-holo-holo-kai, had come down for Luu-kia, carrying a net. They threw their net over the water and the child floated into it. They thought they had a great fish. They carried the net up on the beach and found the boy. It was a little dark, and hard to see what they were catching. One called to the other, "What have we caught this morning?" The other said: "I thought we had a great fish, but this is a child. I will take this child to my home." The other said, "No—This is a fish." So they had a quarrel until the sun rose. Then they went up to the village.

Ka-holo-holo-uka told his wife, "We have a child." Then he told her how they had caught Lei-makani. They talked loudly. This chiefess heard their noisy clamor and asked her servant, "What's the trouble with these noisy ones?" They told her and she wanted that child brought to her, and commanded Maile-lau-lii (Small leaf maile) to go and get it. He took it to Luu-kia, who marked its wonderful beauty. She sent for the fishermen to tell her how they got the child. They told her about the fishing.

She wanted to know who were the parents. They said: "We do not know. This may be the child of Haina-kolo, for we know she has disappeared with her child. She may be dead and this may be her boy."

Luu-kia said, "You two take the child, and I will give the name, Lopa-iki-hele-wale [Going without anything]. Then you care for it until it grows up."

They took the child to the land of Opaeloa, as a good place to bring it up. The fishermen said to Luu-kia, "Will you provide food, fish, and clothing?" She said, "Yes." They thought the child would not understand, but it knew all these words. The fisherman and his wife took the child away. Waipio Valley people were surrounded by precipices, but the gods of Waipio watched all the troubles by sending messengers to go over to the upland and follow Haina-kolo.

Ku and Hina and Olopana were burdened by the loss of Haina-kolo and Lei-makani, so they went to the temple at Pakaalana, where the uncles of Ke-au-nini were staying. There they consulted the gods with signs and sorceries.

They sent Ke-au-miki to get some little stones at Kea-au, a place near Haena. His brother said: "Get thirteen stones—seven white and six black. Make them fast in a bundle, so they cannot be lost, then come back by Pana-ewa and get awa which man did not plant, but which was carried by the birds to the trees and planted there. Then return this evening and we will study the signs." Ke-au-miki went up the pali (precipice) and hastened along the top running and leaping and flying over Hamakua to Hilo.

The Hilo palis were nothing to this man as he sped swiftly over the gulches until he came to the Wailuku River guarded by the kupua Pili-a-mo-o, who concealed the path so that none could find it until a price was paid.   The dragon covered the path with its rough skin.

Ke-au-miki stood looking for a path, but could only see what seemed to be pahoehoe lava.   The tail of the dragon was like a kukui-tree-trunk lying in the water.   He saw the tail switching and rising up to strike him.   Then he knew that this was a kupua.   The tail almost struck him on the head.   He called to Kahuli in Kuai-he-lani, who sent a mighty wind and hurled aside the waters, caught up the body of the dragon and let it fall, smashing it on the rocks, breaking the beds of lava.

Then Ke-au-miki rushed over the river and up the precipices, speeding along to Pa-ai-ie, where the long ohia point of Pana-ewa is found, then turned toward the sea and went to Haena, to the place where the little stones aala-manu are found.   He picked up the stones and ran to Pana-ewa and got the awa hanging on the tree, tied up the awa and stones and hurried back. He crossed the gulch at Konolii and met a man, Lolo-ka-eha, who tried to take the awa away from him.   He was a robber.   When they came face to face, Ke-au-miki caught the man with his hand, hurled him over the precipice and killed him.   When he saw that this man was dead, he ran as swiftly as the wind until he met a very beautiful woman, Wai-puna-lei.   She saw him and asked him to be her husband, but he would not stop. He crossed Hilo boundaries to Hama-kua, to the place where the trees used for kapa were growing, as the sun was going down over the palis. He came to the temple door and laid down his burden.

Then Ke-au-kai said: "This is my word to all the people: Prepare the awa while I take the little stones, pour awa into a cup: I will cover it up and we will watch the signs. If, while I chant, the bubbles on the awa come to the left side, we will find Haina-kolo. If they go to the right, she is fully lost. Let all the people keep silence; no noise, no running about, no sleep-ing. Watch all the signs and the clouds in the heavens."

Then he chanted:

> "O Ku and Kane and Kanaloa,
> Let the magic power come.
> Amama ua noa.
> Tabu is lifted from
> My bird-catching place for food.
> You are a stranger, I am a resident.
> Let the friend be taken care of.
> United is the earth of the tabu woman. Amama."

The bubbles stood on the right side, and the priest said, "We shall never find Haina-kolo; the gods have gone away." Olopana said: "I am much troubled for my brother and sister, and that child I wanted for the chief of this land. I

do not understand why these things have come
to us."

All the people were silent, weeping softly, but
Ke-au-kai and his brother were not troubled, for
they knew their chief and wife were in the care
of the aumakuas.

When Lei-makani had grown up, Luu-kia took
him as her husband. He went surf-riding daily.
She was very jealous of Maile, who would often
go surf-riding with him. Lei-makani did not
care for her, for he knew she was a sister of his
mother although she had a child by him. One
day, when he went with Maile, Luu-kia was
angry and caught that child and killed it by
dashing it against a stone.

The servants went down to the beach, waiting
for Lei-makani to come to land. Then they told
him about the death of his child and their fear
for him if he went up to the house with Maile.
Lei-makani left his surf-board and went to the
house weeping, and found the child's body by
the stone. He took a piece of kapa and wrapped
it up, carrying the broken body down to a fountain, where he cleansed it and offered chants and
incantations until the child became alive. His
mother, Haina-kolo, heard the following chants
and came to her son, for the voice was carried to
her by kupuas who had magic powers. The
child's name was Lono-kai. He wrapped it again

in soft warm kapas and chanted while he washed
the child, naming the fountain Kama-ahala (a
child has passed away):

> "Kama-ahala smells of the blood;
> The sick smell of the blood rises.
> Washed away in the earth is the blood;
> Hard is the red blood
> Warmed by the heat of the heavens,
> Laid out under the shining sky.
> Lono-kai-o-lohia is dead."

Then the voice of the child was heard in a low
moan from the bundle, saying, "Lono-kai-o-
lohia [Lono possessed of the Ala spirit] is alive."
The father heard the voice and softly uttered
another chant:

> "In the silence
> Has been heard the gods of the night;
> What is this wailing over us?
> Wailing for the death of
> Lono, the spirit of the sea—dead!"

The voice came again from the kapas, "Lono,
the spirit of the sea, is alive." Lei-makani's
love for his child was overflowing, and again he
uttered an incantation to his own parents:

> "O Ku, the father!
> O Hina, the mother!
> Olopana was the first-born;
> Haina-kolo, the sister, was born:
> Haina-kolo and Ke-au-nini were the parents:
> Lei-makani was the child:
> I am Lei-makani, the child of Haina-kolo,
> The sacred woman of Waipio's precipices;
> My mother is living among the ripe halas;*

* Pandanus adoratissimus.

> For us was the fruit of the uhi;
> I was found by the fisherman;
> I am the child of the pali hula-anu;
> I was cared for by one of my family
> Inland at Opaeloa;
> They gave me the name Lopa-iki-hele-wale
> [Little lazy fellow having nothing];
> But I am Lei-makani—you shall hear it."

His heart was heavy with longing for his mother, and the gods of the wind, the wind brothers, took his plaintive love-chant to the ears of Haina-kolo, who had wandered in her insanity, but was now free from her craze and had become herself. She followed that voice over the precipices and valleys to the top of a precipice. Standing there and looking down she saw her child and grandchild below, and she chanted:

> "Thy voice I have heard
> Softly echoed by the pali,
> Wailing against the pali;
> Thy voice, my child beloved;
> My child, indeed;
> My child, when the cloud hung over
> And the rainbow light was above us,
> That day when we floated together
> When the sea was breaking my heart;
> My child of the cape of Ka-ia,
> When the sun was hanging above us.
> Where have I been?
> Tell Ke-au-nini-ula-o-ka-lani;
> I was in the midst of the sea
> With the child of our love;
> My child, my little child,
> Where are you?   Oh, come back!"

Then she went down the precipice and met her son holding his child in his arms, and wailed:

> "My lord from the fogs of the inland,
> From the precipices fighting the wind,
> Striking down along the ridges;
> My child, with the voice of a bird,
> Echoed by the precipice of Pakohi,
> Shaking and dancing on inaccessible places,
> Laughing out on the broken waters
> Where we were floating in danger;
> There I loved dearly your voice
> Fighting with waves
> While the fierce storm was above us
> Seen by your many gods
> Who dwell in the shining sky—
> Auwe for us both!"

They waited a little while, until the time when Lono-kai became strong again. Then they went up to the village.

Haina-kolo had run into the forest, her wet pa-u torn off, no clothing left. Her long hair was her cloak, clothing her from head to foot. She wandered until cold, then dressed herself with leaves. As her right senses returned she made warm garments of leaves and ate fruits of the forest. When they came to the village they met the people who knew Haina-kolo. She dwelt there until Lono-kai grew up. He and his father looked like twins, having great resemblance, people told them, to Ke-au-nini. The boy asked, "Where is my grandfather, Ke-au-nini?" Lei-makani said: "I never saw your grandfather. He was very tabu and sacred. He killed his own

father, Ku-aha-ilo, god of the heavens. I know
by my mana [spirit power] that he is with the
daughters of Milu." The boy said: "I must go
and find him. I will go in my spirit body, leaving this human body. You must not forbid the
journey." Ke-au-kai, the priest, said: "You cannot find him unless you learn what to do before
you go. Those chiefs of Milu have many sports
and games. I tell you these things must be
learned before you go into that land. If you
are able to win against the spirits of that place
you can get your grandfather."

All the chiefs aided the boy to acquire skill in
all sports. They went to the fields of Paaohau.
Nuanua, the most skilful teacher of hula, taught
him to dance. The highest chiefs and chiefesses
went with him to help, taking their retinues with
them. Lei-makani said: "The knowledge of
sports is the means by which you will catch your
grandfather. Now be careful. Do not be stingy
with food. Give to others and take care of the
people."

They went up in a great company, and Haina-
kolo wondered at the beauty of the boy, and asked
why they were travelling. Lono-kai told them
the reason for his journey and desire to see the
field of sports.

Nuanua, the hula teacher, sent his assistants
to get all kinds of leaves and flowers used in the

hula, then sent for a black pig to be used as
an omen. If it ran to Lono-kai, he would become a good dancer; if not, he would fail. The
pig went to him. The priest offered this prayer:

"Laka is living where the forest leaves are trembling,
The ghost-god of dancers above and below,
From the boundary of the North to the place most southern:
O Laka, your altar is covered with leaves,
The dancing leaves of the ieie vine;
This offering of leaves is the labor of the gods,
The gods of your family, Pele and Hiiaka;
The women living in warm winds come here for the toil,
And this labor of ours is learning your dance.
Tabu laid down; tabu lifted. Amama ua noa [we are through]!"

The priest lifted his eyes, and the pig was seen
lying at the foot of the boy. Then he commenced
teaching the boy the kilu and the first dance.
They were thirty days learning the dances, and
the boy learned all those his teachers knew.

Then they went around Hawaii, studying the
dances. He was told to go back and get all the
new ideas and seek the gods to learn their newest
dance, for theirs differed from those of his teachers. He was to seek this knowledge in dreams.
Lei-makani said: "Your teachers have shown
you the slow way; if that is all you know, you
will win fame, but not victory. You must learn
from the gods." Lono-kai again went to Hamakua with his companions and learned how to play
konane, the favorite game of Ke-au-nini. The
teacher said, "I have taught you all I know

inside and outside, as I would not teach the other young chiefs." The boy said to him, "There is one thing more,—give offerings to the gods that they may teach us in our dreams newer and better ways."

So they waited quietly, offering sacrifices. The priests told him to set apart a pig while he made a prayer. If the pig died during the prayer, he would not forget anything learned. The boy laid his right hand on the pig and began to pray:

> "Here is a pig, an offering to the gods.
> O Lono in the Under-world, Lono in the sky:
> O Kane, who makes not-to-be-broken laws,
> Kane in the darkness, Kane in the hot wind,
> Kane of the generations, Kane of the thunder,
> Kane in the whirlwind and the storm:
> Here is labor—labor of the gods.
> My body is alive for you!
> Filled up is the Nuu-pule.
> My prayer is for those you hold dear
> O Laka, come with knowledge and magic power!
> Laka, dancing in the moving forest leaves
> Of the mountain ridges and the valleys,
> Return and bestow the knowledge
> Of Pele and Hiiaka, the guardians of the wind,
> Knowing the multitude of the gods of the night,
> Knowing Aukele-nui-aku in the Under-world.
> O people of the night,
> Here is the pig, the offering!
> Come with knowledge, magic power, and safety.
> Amama ua noa."

Then the boy lifted his hand and the pig lay silent in death. Then came thunder shaking the earth, and lightning flashing in flames, and a storm breaking in red rain. Mists came and the shadows of the thousands of gods of Ke-au-nini fell upon the boy. The teachers and friends sat in perfect silence for a long time. The storm was beating outside, and the boy was overcome with weariness and wondered at the silence of his friends.

Rainbow colors were about him, and the people were awed by their fears and sat still until evening came. Then the teacher asked the boy if he saw what had been done in the darkness resting over him, and if he could explain to them. The boy said, "I do not understand you; perhaps my teacher can explain."

Nuanua said: "I am growing old and have never seen such things above any one learning the dance. You have come to me modestly, like one of the common people, when I should have gone to you, and now the gods show your worth and power and their favor."

Then he took a piece of wood from the hula altar which was covered with leaves and flowers, and, putting it in a cup of awa, shook it, and looked, and said to the boy: "This is the best I can do for you. Now the gods will take you in their care." Then he poured awa into cups, passing them to all the people as he chanted incantations, all the company clapping their hands. Then they drank. But the boy's cup was drunk by the eepas of Po (gnomes of the night). So the company feasted and the night became calm. Lono-kai that night left his friends with Nuanua and journeyed on. He waited some days and then told Lei-makani he thought he was ready. He said: "Yes, I have heard about your success, but I will see what you can do. We will wait another ten days before you go." Then for two days all the people of Waipio brought their offerings. They built a great lanai, and feated. Lei-makani told the people that he had called them together to see the wonderful power in the sports of the boy. So the boy stood up and chanted:

> "O Kuamu-amu [the little people of the clouds of the sky],
> The alii thronging in crowds from Kuai-he-lani,
> On the shoulders of Moana-liha, divided at the waters,
> Divided at the waters of the heavy mist,
> And the rain coming from the skies,
> And the storm rushing inland.
> Broken into mists are the falls of the mountains,—
> Mists that bathe the buds of the flowers,
> Opening the buds below the precipices.
> Arise, O beloved one!"

Ke-au-nini heard this chant, even down in Po, while he was sporting with the eepas of Milu, while his spirit body was with his friend Popo-alaea. He repeated the same chant, and the ghosts all rejoiced and laughed, and Laka leaped to his side and danced before him. They had the same sports as the noted ones on Hawaii. Lono-kai danced in magic power before all the

people until the time came for him to go along
the path of his visions of the night. All omens
and signs had been noted and were found to be
favorable. One of the old priests told the people
to make known their thought about the best
path for the young chief, but they were silent.
Then Moli-lele, an old priest who had the spirit
of the unihipilis resting upon him, said: "I know
that there will be many troubles. Cold and
fierce winds come over the sea. Low tides come
in the morning. The land of Kane-huna-moku
rises in the coral surf." He chanted:

> "Dead is this chief of ours,
> Caught as a bird strikes a fish;
> The foam of surf waves rises up,
> Smiting and driving below.
> No sorcerer of the land is there,
> Where the coral reef labors,
> And the rock-eating Hina of the far-off sea."

The chiefs began to wail, but lightning was in
the eyes of the boy and his face was filled with
anger at this word of the old priest. Then
another priest arose and said: "O chiefs and
people, I have seen the path to the Under-world,
and it is not right for this young man to go. His
body is human and easily captured by the ghosts.
He might be safe if he could get the body of the
one he seeks. There are fierce guardians of the
path who will make war on whoever comes in
the flesh."

Then Kalei, another priest, said: "I know their world. I saw the stars this morning, and they told me that the path was stopped against this chief by broken coral and the bones of the dead. The tabu-children of Hina are swimming in the sea. I will prove the danger by this awa cup. If the bubbles of the awa poured in go to the right, he can go. If to the left, he must stay." This he did uttering incantations, but bubbles covered all the surface.

Then the priests advised the young chief to stay and eat the fat of the land. Then Hae-hae, the great chief, said, "We have come to point out a path, if we can, and to make quiet and peaceful that way into Po." He instituted new omens, and showed that the young chief would be successful, but he would have many difficulties to overcome.

Lono-kai arose and said: "The words of these chiefs were twisted. I will go after the spirit-body of my grandfather, as I have sworn to do. My word is fast. I will go to the land where my grandfather stays."

The priests who had tried to terrify Lono-kai were his enemies, and would oppose his journey, and he wanted them killed, but Lei-makani would not permit it. Ku also quieted him with patient words, and he ceased from anger and told them he must prepare at once to go.

Lei-makani had a double canoe made ready, and selected a number of strong men to accompany the young chief. Lono-kai would not have any of these men, but went out early in the morning, took a cup of awa to the temple nearby and chanted his genealogical mele.

Thunder and lightning and heavy wind and rain attended his visit to the temple. He returned to his parents and told them to wait for him thirty days. If a mist was over all the land they might wait and watch ten days more, and if the mist continued, another ten, when he would return with thunder and lightning to meet his friends. But if the voices of the sea were strong at Kumukahi, with mist resting on Opaeloa and rain on Puu-o-ka-polei, then he would be dead.

He took his feather cloak and war weapons from his grandparents, and feather helmet, and went out. He bade his parents farewell, took a coconut-husk canoe and went down to the sea. The waves rose high, pounding the face of the coast precipices. Lei-makani ran down to bring Lono-kai back, but according to the proverb he caught the hand of the chiefess who lives in the land of Nowhere. The boy had disappeared.

Out in the sea Lono-kai was tossing in the high waves, passing all the islands, even to the land Niihau. There he met the great watchman of Kuai-he-lani called Honu (the turtle). He came quietly near the head. Honu asked, "Where are you going?" Lono-kai said: "You speak as if you alone had the right to the sea. You are a humpbacked turtle; you shall become a great round stone." Then the turtle began to slap its fins on the sea, raising waves high as precipices. Five times forty he struck the sea with mighty force, looking for the destruction of the chief as the waves passed over him. But Lono-kai waited until the turtle became tired, thinking the chief dead. As the waters became calm the chief raised his club and struck the right flapper of the turtle, destroying its power.

Then the left fin beat the sea into foam, but Lono-kai waited and broke that fin also; then he broke the back of the turtle into little pieces and went on his way. Soon the ocean grew fierce again. Huge waves came, and whirlwinds. He saw something red in the great sea—a kupua of the ocean. The name of this enemy was Ea, a great red turtle, who crawled out and asked where he was going. Lono-kai said: "What right have you to question me? Have I questioned your right to go on the sea?"

Ea said: "This is not your place. I will kill you. You shall be food for me to eat. When you are dead I will go and kill the watchman who let you come into this tabu-sea of my chief."

"Who is your chief?" asked Lono-kai. Ea replied: "Hina-kekai [the calabash for boiling water], the daughter of Pii-moi. Now I will kill you."

Then Ea began to strike the water with his right fin, throwing the water up on all sides in mighty waves, expecting to overthrow Lono-kai and his boat. When he rested to see the result of this battle his fin was on the surface, and the chief struck it and broke it.

Then in another fight, when head and fin were lifted to destroy the boat, Lono-kai struck the neck and broke it, so killing his enemy.

Now he thought all his troubles were over and he could go safely on his way.

But soon there lay before him a new enemy, floating on the sea, a very long thing, like a long stick. He approached and saw that it was like the fin of a shark, but as he came nearer he observed the smooth skin of a long eel. Lifting its head and looking right at him, the eel said: "O, proud man, you are here where you have no business to be. I will mix you with my awa and eat you now." Then he struck at Lono-kai with his tail and hit his eyes and knocked him down, then, thinking Lono-kai was dead, he turned his head to the boat to catch the body, but Lono-kai, leaping up on the head of the eel, holding his boat with one hand and his club with the other, struck the head with the magic club,

breaking the bones.   Fire came out of the broken
head, the eel falling into pieces which became
islands of fire in the midst of which appeared a
very beautiful woman who asked him whence he
came, and why.

He told her he was from Hawaii and was going
to Kuai-he-lani and would kill her, for he thought
she was a mo-o, or dragon-woman. He said,
"You tried to kill me, O woman, and now
you must stay and become the fire oven of the
ocean." He asked her name. She said to him:
"This kupua was Waka, the dragon of the rough
head, and I have escaped from his body. I want
you now for my husband, and I will accompany
you on your journey."

Lono-kai told her, "This would not be right,
but when I return, if I come this way, you shall
be mine." She said, "My ruler will kill me, for
I have been sent to guard this place." Lono-kai
asked, "Who is your ruler?" "Hina-kekai, she
will kill me. You belong to the Ku-aha-ilo family, which is a very strong family. Therefore we
have been watching for you for our chiefess."

Lono-kai told her to go to his land and wait
for him. He would be her husband. She must
wait there without fault until his return. Then
he went away. Waka did not know whence this
chief came, so she went to Oahu and landed at
Laiewai.   There she awaited her husband.

Lono-kai went on to the land of Kuai-he-lani, where he landed and hid his boat among the vines on the beach. He went to the temple where the body of his grandfather lay, clean and beautiful in death. He could not see any door or break in the body for the escape of the spirit.

Then he struck the earth with his magic war-club until a great hole opened. He looked down and saw a large house and many people moving around below. He knew that the spirit of his grandfather was there. He went down and looked about, but the people had disappeared. The remains of a great feast were there. He stood at the door looking in, when two men appeared and welcomed him with an "Aloha," and told him he must have come from the land above, for there was no man like him in that place. They advised him to make his path back into that land from whence he had come, for if the king of the Under-world saw him he would be killed. Lono-kai asked, "Who is your king?" They told him, "Milu." "What does he do?" "Our king dances for Popo-alaea and Ke-au-nini." Lono-kai went with the men to see the sports. They tried to persuade him not to go, but he was very obstinate and asked them to hide him. They said, "If we do this and you are discovered we shall be destroyed."

He told them the reason of his coming and

asked their help, and said when he had his grandfather they could follow him into the Upper-
world. They went to a house which was large
and beautiful. They entered and saw the chiefs
playing kilu. After a long time Lono-kai began
to make his presence known. Popo-alaea was
winning. Then Ke-au-nini chanted:

> "The multitude of those below give greeting
> To the friends of the inland forest of Puna;
> We praise the restfulness of our home;
> The leaves and divine flowers of that place."

Lono-kai chanted the same words as an echo
of Ke-au-nini. Silence fell on the group, and
Milu cried out: "Who is the disturber of our
sport? We must find him and kill him." They
began the search, but could not find any one
and at last resumed their games. Popo-alaea
chanted:

> "I welcome back my friend,
> The great shadow of Waimea,
> Where stands the milo-tree * in the gentle breeze,
> And the ohia-tree. You know the place."

Ke-au-nini sang the same chant. Then Lono-
kai echoed it very softly and sweetly. All said
this last voice was the best. Milu again caused
a search to be made, but found nothing. The
two men hid Lono-kai by a post of the house.

The group returned to the sports. Soon Milu
changed the game to hula. Ke-au-nini stood up
to dance and began his chant:

* Thespesia populnea.

> "Aloha to our houses without friends.
> The path goes inland to Papalakamo;
> Come now and enter!
> Outside is the trouble, the storm,
> And there you meet the cold."

The people around were striking the spirit drums. Then Lono-kai chanted:

> "Established is the honor of Ke-au-nini
> (Noteworthy is the name),
> Lifted up to the high heaven;
> I am the child of Lei-makani,
> I am Lono from the sunrise place, Hae-o-hae:
> I have come after thee, my father;
> We must return. Where are you?"

Ke-au-nini could not stand up to dance when he heard the voice of his grandchild, for his love overpowered him. He looked up and saw the form of the young chief leaping into the place prepared for the hula and standing there before the chief. The people rose up in great confusion. Lono-kai caught the spirit of Ke-au-nini and put it in a coconut-shell. He leaped past the ghosts, and ran very swiftly out of the house.

Some of the people saw him lay hands on Ke-au-nini, and cried out: "Oh, the husband of our chiefess! Oh, the husband of our chiefess! He has taken the husband of our chiefess!" But they did not see Lono-kai go out. The two men who had aided Lono-kai went out as soon as he leaped into the hula place. They hurried along the path toward freedom, but Lono-kai soon overtook them. Milu called to his people to hasten and capture and kill the one who had stolen Ke-au-nini. They saw the two men with Lono-kai, and pursued rapidly, but could not overtake them. The fugitives were very near the opening to the world above. When Lono-kai saw that the pursuers were almost upon him he whirled his magic war-club and struck the ground, making a great hole into which the spirits fell one over the other.

Lono-kai and the two watchmen went up the cave opening by which he had gone down into the land of Milu. Dawn was breaking as they ran into the temple at Kuai-he-lani, where the body of Ke-au-nini was lying. Lono-kai pushed the spirit into the hollow of the foot and held the foot fast, shaking it until the spirit had gone to the very ends of the body and life had returned.

When Ke-au-nini was fully restored, Lono-kai asked him if he could help restore to their bodies the two spirits who had aided him in escaping. Ke-au-nini evidently did not remember anything of his life in the Under-world, for he did not know these ghosts and thought he had been asleep from the time he entered the temple and fell down in weariness. Lono-kai thought they could not find the bodies, but Ke-au-nini put the ghosts in coconuts and carried them up into the forest to one of his ancestors who knew the bodies from which these ghosts had come. Thus they were restored and had a long and happy life in their former home.

Lono-kai told his grandfather they must return to Hawaii to meet all the friends.

For thirty days mists covered Hawaii and there was thunder and lightning and earthquakes. Then Lono-kai said to Ke-au-nini: "To-morrow we must go to Hawaii. We must have the appropriate ceremonies for cleansing and taking food." Ke-au-nini said: "Yes, I have been a long time in the adopted land of Milu, and my eyes are dimmed and my thought is dazed with the dance of the restless spirits of the night. We must wait until I have performed all the cleansing ceremonies, made offerings and incantations. Prayers must be said for my return to life. Then we will go."

They attended to all the temple rites, and the marks of death were washed away. The body was cleansed, the eyes made clear, so strength and joy returned into the body. Then Ke-au-nini said: "I am ready. I see a multitude of birds circling around Kaula. There is evil toward Hawaii."

They again went into the temple and slept until very early the next morning. Then they took their coconut-husk canoes, each holding his own in his hand, and went down to the edge

of the sea and stood there, each pointing the nose
of his boat toward Waipio.

None of the people awoke until they landed.
They pulled the boats upon the beach and went
to their temple. As they came to the door of the
temple, drums beat like rolling thunder. Then
the sun arose, the mists all vanished from Hawaii.
The people awoke and understood that their
chiefs had returned. They ran out of their
houses shouting and rejoicing. Olopana commanded the chiefs and the people to prepare all
kinds of sweet food and gifts and things for a very
great luau. When this was done they feasted
sixty days and returned to their homes.

Lei-makani became the ruler of Hawaii.
Lono-kai-o-lohia was honored by his father. All
of the chiefs in that generation were noted
throughout the islands.

It was said that there was a beautiful chiefess
of Molokai who wanted to find a young chief of
Hawaii for her husband, so she sent her kahu, or
guardian, and servants to make the journey
while she went back to her sleeping-place and
dreamed of a very fine young chief shining like

the sun and surrounded by all the colors of the rainbow. Then she awoke and found no one, but she loved that spirit-body which she had seen in her dreams, so she arose and went down to the beach and told her guardian to make haste and reach Hawaii that day.

When the kahu heard her call, he put forth all his power and uttered the proper incantations. He sped through the waters like a skimming bird, passed the great precipices near Waipio, and soon after dawn landed on the beautiful beach.

The people had not yet come from their homes for the work of the day. He went up to the village and came near the house of Lei-makani. A watchman asked where he was from and the purpose of his journey. He said: "I am a stranger from Molokai, a messenger from my chiefess, who seeks a husband of high rank equal to her own. She has no one worthy to be her husband."

The Waipio chief said: "We have a splendid young chief, but there is no one his equal in rank and beauty. You could not ask for him."

Then Lei-makani heard the noise and came out and asked about this conversation. His watchman told him that this man was from Molokai.

Lei-makani asked the man to approach. The Molokai chief thought that Lei-makani was the

handsomest man he had ever seen. Ke-au-kai
came out of the temple and looked upon the
stranger and asked why he had come.

When he learned that the man sought a husband for his chiefess, he advised him to return
lest he should meet death at the hands of the
watchman, but the man would not go away.

After a time the chiefs of Waipio came before
Lei-makani. The Molokai chief explained his
errand, and praised his chiefess, and said that he
was willing to be killed and cooked in an oven if
she were not as beautiful and of as high rank
as he had told them. Lono-kai at that moment
entered the assembly, and the stranger cried out:
"This man is the husband for my chiefess. Her
tabu rank is the same as the tabu rank of this
fine young chief. No others in all the islands are
like these two. It would be glorious for them to
meet." Lono-kai said, "You return at once and
make preparation, and I will come in the evening."

The kahu returned to Molokai, but the chiefess
saw him coming back alone and became very
angry, her eyes flashing with wrath because he
had not brought the young chief with him. She
screamed out, "Where is the value of your journey, if you return without my husband?"

"Wait a little," the guardian said gently,
"until you hear about what I have seen upon

Hawaii. I have found the one you wanted. We must get ready to meet your husband, for the young chief is coming here this evening. When you meet, the love of each of you will be great toward the other."

She ordered all Molokai to prepare for a great feast commencing that evening. Messengers ran swiftly, people and chiefs hastened their labors, and by evening vast quantities of food had been prepared.

Lono-kai took his coconut-husk boat and came over the sea like a bird skimming the water.

As the sun sank and the evening shadows fell, the two young people met and delighted in each other's beauty. Then they were married in the midst of all the people of Molokai.

XVIII

THE BRIDE FROM THE UNDER-WORLD

A Legend of the Kalakaua Family

KU, one of the most widely known gods of the Pacific Ocean, was thought by the Hawaiians to have dwelt as a mortal for some time on the western side of the island Hawaii. Here he chose a chiefess by the name of Hina as his wife, and to them were born two children. When he withdrew from his residence among men he left a son on the uplands of the district of North Kona, and a daughter on the seashore of the same district. The son, Hiku-i-kana-hele (Hiku of the forest), lived with his mother. The daughter, Kewalu, dwelt under the care of guardian chiefs and priests by a temple, the ruined walls of which are standing even to the present day. Here she was carefully protected and perfected in all arts pertaining to the very high chiefs. Hiku-of-the-Forest was not accustomed to go to the sea. His life was developed among the forests along the western slopes of the great mountains of Hawaii. Here he learned the wisdom of his mother and of the chiefs and priests under whose care he was placed. To him were given many of the supernatural powers of his father. His mother guarded him from the knowledge that he had a sister and kept him from going to the temple by the side of which she had her home.

Hiku was proficient in all the feats of manly strength and skill upon which chiefs of the highest rank prided themselves. None of the chiefs of the inland districts could compare with him in symmetry of form, beauty of countenance, and skill in manly sports.

The young chief noted the sounds of the forest and the rushing winds along the sides of the mountains. Sometimes, like storm voices, he heard from far off the beat of the surf along the coral reef. One day he heard a noise like the flapping of the wings of many birds. He looked toward the mountain, but no multitude of his feathered friends could be found. Again the same sound awakened his curiosity. He now learned that it came from the distant seashore far below his home on the mountain-side.

Hiku-of-the-Forest called his mother and together they listened as again the strange sound from the beach rose along the mountain gulches and was echoed among the cliffs.

"E Hiku," said the mother, "that is the clapping of the hands of a large number of men and women. The people who live by the sea are very much pleased and are expressing their great delight in some wonderful deed of a great chief."

Day after day the rejoicing of the people was heard by the young chief. At last he sent a trusty retainer to learn the cause of the tumult. The messenger reported that he had found certain tabu surf waters of the Kona beach and had seen a very high chiefess who alone played with her surf-board on the incoming waves. Her beauty surpassed that of any other among all the people, and her skill in riding the surf was wonderful, exceeding that of any one whom the people had ever seen, therefore the multitude gathered from near and far to watch the marvelous deeds of the beautiful woman. Their pleasure was so great that when they clapped their hands the sound was like the voices of many thunder-storms.

The young chief said he must go down and see this beautiful maiden. The mother knew that this chiefess of such great beauty must be Kewalu, the sister of Hiku. She feared that trouble would come to Kewalu if her more powerful brother should find her and take her in marriage, as was the custom among the people. The omens which had been watched concerning the children in their infancy had predicted many serious troubles. But the young man could not be restrained. He was determined to see the wonderful woman.

He sent his people to gather the nuts of the kukui, or candlenut-tree, and crush out the oil and prepare it for anointing his body. He had never used a surf-board, but he commanded his servants to prepare the best one that could be made. Down to the seashore Hiku went with his retainers, down to the tabu place of the beautiful Kewalu.

He anointed his body with the kukui oil until it glistened like the polished leaves of trees; then taking his surf-board he went boldly to the tabu surf waters of his sister. The people stood in amazed silence, expecting to see speedy punishment meted out to the daring stranger. But the gods of the sea favored Hiku. Hiku had never been to the seaside and had never learned the arts of those who were skilful in the waters. Nevertheless as he entered the water he carried the surf-board more royally than any chief the people had ever known. The sunlight shone in splendor upon his polished body when he stood on the board and rode to the shore on the crests of the highest surf waves, performing wonderful feats by his magic power. The joy of the multitude was unbounded, and a mighty storm of noise was made by the clapping of their hands.

Kewalu and her maidens had left the beach before the coming of Hiku and were resting in their grass houses in a grove of coconut-trees near the heiau. When the great noise made by the people aroused her she sent one of her friends to learn the cause of such rejoicing. When she learned that an exceedingly handsome chief of the highest rank was sporting among her tabu waters she determined to see him.

So, calling her maidens, she went down to the seashore and first saw Hiku on the highest crest of the rolling surf. She decided at once that she had never seen a man so comely, and Hiku, surf-riding to the shore, felt that he had never dreamed of such grace and beauty as marked the maiden who was coming to welcome him.

When Kewalu came near she took the wreath of rare and fragrant flowers which she wore and coming close to him threw it around his shoulders as a token to all the people that she had taken him to be her husband.

Then the joy of the people surpassed all the pleasure of all the days before, for they looked upon the two most beautiful beings they had ever seen and believed that these two would make glad each other's lives.

Thus Hiku married his sister, Kewalu, according to the custom of that time, because she was the only one of all the people equal to him in rank and beauty, and he alone was fitted to stand in her presence.

For a long time they lived together, sometimes sporting among the highest white crests of storm-tossed surf waves, sometimes enjoying the guessing and gambling games in which the Hawaiians of all times have been very expert, sometimes chanting meles and genealogies and telling marvelous stories of sea and forest, and sometimes feasting and resting under the trees surrounding their grass houses.

Hiku at last grew weary of the life by the sea. He wanted the forest on the mountain and the cold, stimulating air of the uplands. But he did not wish to take his sister-wife with him. Perhaps the omens of their childhood had revealed danger to Kewalu if she left her home by the sea. Whenever he tried to steal away from her she would rush to him and cling to him, persuading him to wait for new sports and joys.

One night Hiku rose up very quietly and passed out into the darkness. As he began to climb toward the uplands the leaves of the trees rustled loudly in welcome. The night birds circled around him and hastened him on his way, but Kewalu was awakened. She called for Hiku. Again and again she called, but Hiku had gone. She heard his footsteps as his eager tread shook the ground. She heard the branches breaking

as he forced his way through the forests.   Then
she hastened after him and her plaintive cry was
louder and clearer than the voices of the night
birds.

> "E Hiku, return!   E Hiku, return!
>   O my love, wait for Kewalu!
>   Hiku goes up the hills;
>   Very hard is this hill, O Hiku!
>   O Hiku, my beloved!"

But Hiku by his magic power sent thick fogs
and mists around her.   She was blinded and
chilled, but she heard the crashing of the branches
and ferns as Hiku forced his way through them,
and she pressed on, still calling:

"E Hiku, beloved, return to Kewalu."

Then the young chief threw the long flexible
vines of the ieie down into the path.   They
twined around her feet and made her stumble as
she tried to follow him.   The rain was falling all
around her, and the way was very rough and
hard.   She slipped and fell again and again.

The ancient chant connected with the legend
says:

> "Hiku is climbing up the hill.
>   Branches and vines are in the way,
>   And Kewalu is begging him to stop.
>   Rain-drops are walking on the leaves.
>   The flowers are beaten to the ground.
>   Hopeless the quest, but Kewalu is calling:
>   'E Hiku, beloved!   Let us go back together.'"

Her tears, mingled with the rain, streamed
down her cheeks.   The storm wet and destroyed

the kapa mantle which she had thrown around her as she hurried from her home after Hiku. In rags she tried to force her way through the tangled undergrowth of the uplands, but as she crept forward step by step she stumbled and fell again into the cold wet mass of ferns and grasses. Then the vines crept up around her legs and her arms and held her, but she tore them loose and forced her way upward, still calling. She was bleeding where the rough limbs of the trees had torn her delicate flesh. She was so bruised and sore from the blows of the bending branches that she could scarcely creep along.

At last she could no longer hear the retreating footsteps of Hiku. Then, chilled and desolate and deserted, she gave up in despair and crept back to the village. There she crawled into the grass house where she had been so happy with her brother Hiku, intending to put an end to her life.

The ieie vines held her arms and legs, but she partially disentangled herself and wound them around her head and neck. Soon the tendrils grew tight and slowly but surely choked the beautiful chiefess to death. This was the first suicide in the records of Hawaiian mythology. As the body gradually became lifeless the spirit crept upward to the lua-uhane, the door by which it passed out of the body into the spirit world. This "spirit-door" is the little hole in the corner of the eye. Out of it the spirit is thought to creep slowly as the body becomes cold in death. The spirit left the cold body a prisoner to the tangled vines, and slowly and sadly journeyed to Milu, the Under-world home of the ghosts of the departed.

The lust of the forest had taken possession of Hiku. He felt the freedom of the swift birds who had been his companions in many an excursion into the heavily shaded depths of the forest jungles. He plunged with abandon into the whirl and rush of the storm winds which he had called to his aid to check Kewalu. He was drunken with the atmosphere which he had breathed throughout his childhood and young manhood. When he thought of Kewalu he was sure that he had driven her back to her home by the temple, where he could find her when once more he should seek the seashore.

He had only purposed to stay a while on the uplands, and then return to his sister-wife.

His father, the god Ku, had been watching him and had also seen the suicide of the beautiful Kewalu. He saw the spirit pass down to the kingdom of Milu, the home of the ghosts. Then he called Hiku and told him how heedless and thoughtless he had been in his treatment of

Kewalu, and how in despair she had taken her life, the spirit going to the Under-world.

Hiku, the child of the forest, was overcome with grief. He was ready to do anything to atone for the suffering he had caused Kewalu, and repair the injury.

Ku told him that only by the most daring effort could he hope to regain his loved bride. He could go to the Under-world, meet the ghosts and bring his sister back, but this could only be done at very great risk to himself, for if the ghosts discovered and captured him they would punish him with severest torments and destroy all hope of returning to the Upper-world.

Hiku was determined to search the land of Milu and find his bride and bring her back to his Kona home by the sea. Ku agreed to aid him with the mighty power which he had as a god, nevertheless it was absolutely necessary that Hiku should descend alone and by his own wit and skill secure the ghost of Kewalu.

Hiku prepared a coconut-shell full of oil made from decayed kukui nuts. This was very vile and foul smelling. Then he made a long stout rope of ieie vines.

Ku knew where the door to the Under-world was, through which human beings could go down. This was a hole near the seashore in the valley of Waipio on the eastern coast of the island.

Ku and Hiku went to Waipio, descended the precipitous walls of the valley and found the door to the pit of Milu. Milu was the ruler of the Under-world.

Hiku rubbed his body all over with the rancid kukui oil and then gave the ieie vine into the keeping of his father to hold fast while he made his descent into the world of the spirits of the dead. Slowly Ku let the vine down until at last Hiku stood in the strange land of Milu.

No one noticed his coming and so for a little while he watched the ghosts, studying his best method of finding Kewalu. Some of the ghosts were sleeping; some were gambling and playing the same games they had loved so well while living in the Upper-world; others were feasting and visiting around the poi bowl as they had formerly been accustomed to do.

Hiku knew that the strong odor of the rotten oil would be his best protection, for none of the spirits would want to touch him and so would not discover that he was flesh and blood. Therefore he rubbed his body once more thoroughly with the oil and disfigured himself with dirt. As he passed from place to place searching for Kewalu, the ghosts said, "What a bad-smelling spirit!" So they turned away from him as if he was one of the most unworthy ghosts dwelling in Milu. In the realm of Milu he saw the people in the

game of rolling coconut-shells to hit a post.
Kulioe, one of the spirits, had been playing the
kilu and had lost all his property to the daughter
of Milu and one of her friends. He saw Hiku
and said, "If you are a skilful man perhaps you
should play with these two girls." Hiku said:
"I have nothing. I have only come this day
and am alone." Kulioe bet his bones against
some of the property he had lost. The first
girl threw her cup at the kilu post. Hiku
chanted:

> "Are you known by Papa and Wakea,
>   O eyelashes or rays of the sun?
>   Mine is the cup of kilu."

Her cup did not touch the kilu post before Hiku.
She threw again, but did not touch, while Hiku
chanted the same words. They took a new cup,
but failed.

Hiku commenced swinging the cup and threw.
It glided and twisted around on the floor and
struck the post. This counted five and won the
first bet. Then he threw the cup numbered
twenty, won all the property and gave it back
to Kulioe.

At last he found Kewalu, but she was by the
side of the high chief, Milu, who had seen the
beautiful princess as she came into the Under-
world. More glorious was Kewalu than any
other of all those of noble blood who had ever

descended to Milu. The ghosts had welcomed the spirit of the princess with great rejoicing, and the king had called her at once to the highest place in his court.

She had not been long with the chiefs of Milu before they asked her to sing or chant her mele. The mele was the family song by which any chief made known his rank and the family with which he was connected, whenever he visited chiefs far away from his own home.

Hiku heard the chant and mingled with the multitude of ghosts gathered around the place where the high chiefs were welcoming the spirit of Kewalu.

While Hiku and Kewalu had been living together one of their pleasures was composing and learning to intone a chant which no other among either mortals or spirits should know besides themselves.

While Kewalu was singing she introduced her part of this chant. Suddenly from among the throng of ghosts arose the sound of a clear voice chanting the response which was known by no other person but Hiku.

Kewalu was overcome by the thought that perhaps Hiku was dead and was now among the ghosts, but did not dare to incur the hatred of King Milu by making himself known; or perhaps Hiku had endured many dangers of the lower world by coming even in human form to find her and therefore must remain concealed.

The people around the king, seeing her grief, were not surprised when she threw a mantle around herself and left them to go away alone into the shadows.

She wandered from place to place among the groups of ghosts, looking for Hiku. Sometimes she softly chanted her part of the mele. At last she was again answered and was sure that Hiku was near, but the only one very close was a foul-smelling, dirt-covered ghost from whom she was turning away in despair.

Hiku in a low tone warned her to be very careful and not recognize him, but assured her that he had come in person to rescue her and take her back to her old home where her body was then lying. He told her to wander around and yet to follow him until they came to the ieie vine which he had left hanging from the hole which opened to the Upper-world.

When Hiku came to the place where the vine was hanging he took hold to see if Ku, his father, was still carefully guarding the other end to pull him up when the right signal should be given. Having made himself sure of the aid of the god, he tied the end of the vine into a strong loop and seated himself in it. Then he began to swing back and forth, back and forth, sometimes rising

high and sometimes checking himself and resting
with his feet on the ground.

Kewalu came near and begged to be allowed
to swing, but Hiku would only consent on the
condition that she would sit in his lap.

The ghosts thought that this would be an excellent arrangement and shouted their approval
of the new sport. Then Hiku took the spirit of
Kewalu in his strong arms and began to swing
slowly back and forth, then more and more
rapidly, higher and higher until the people mar-
velled at the wonderful skill. Meanwhile he
gave the signal to Ku to pull them up. Almost
imperceptibly the swing receded from the spirit
world.

All this time Hiku had been gently and lovingly rubbing the spirit of Kewalu and softly
uttering charm after charm so that while they
were swaying in the air she was growing smaller
and smaller. Even the chiefs of Milu had been
attracted to this unusual sport, and had drawn
near to watch the wonderful skill of the strange
foul-smelling ghost.

Suddenly it dawned upon some of the beholders
that the vine was being drawn up to the Upper-
world. Then the cry arose: "He is stealing the
woman!" "He is stealing the woman!"

The Under-world was in a great uproar of
noise. Some of the ghosts were leaping as high

as they could, others were calling for Hiku to return, and others were uttering charms to cause his downfall.

No one could leap high enough to touch Hiku, and the power of all the charms was defeated by the god Ku, who rapidly drew the vine upward.

Hiku succeeded in charming the ghost of Kewalu into the coconut-shell which he still carried. Then stopping the opening tight with his fingers so that the spirit could not escape he brought Kewalu back to the land of mortals.

With the aid of Ku the steep precipices surrounding Waipio Valley were quickly scaled and the journey made to the temple by the tabu surf waters of Kona. Here the body of Kewalu had been lying in state. Here the auwe, or mourning chant, of the retinue of the dead princess could be heard from afar.

Hiku passed through the throngs of mourners, carefully guarding his precious coconut until he came to the feet, cold and stiff in death. Kneeling down he placed the small hole in the end of the shell against the tender spot in the bottom of one of the cold feet.

The spirits of the dead must find their way back little by little through the body from the feet to the eyes, from which they must depart when they bid final farewell to the world. To try to send the spirit back into the body by placing it in the lua-uhane, or "door of the soul," would be to have it where it had to depart from the body rather than enter it.

Hiku removed his finger from the hole in the coconut and uttered the incantations which would allure the ghost into the body. Little by little the soul of Kewalu came back, and the body grew warm from the feet upward, until at last the eyes opened and the soul looked out upon the blessed life restored to it by the skill and bravery of Hiku.

No more troubles arose to darken the lives of the children of Ku. Whether in the forest or by the sea they made the days pleasant for each other until at the appointed time together they entered the shades of Milu as chief and chiefess who could not be separated. It is said that the generations of their children gave many rulers to the Hawaiians, and that the present royal family, the "House of Kalakaua," is the last of the descendants.

PART II

DESCRIPTION

THE DECEIVING OF KEWA

A poem, or mourning chant, of the Maoris of New Zealand has many references to the deeds of their ancestors in Hawaiki, which in this case surely has reference to the Hawaiian Islands. Among the first lines of this poem is the expression, "Kewa was deceived." An explanatory note is given which covers almost two pages of the Journal of the Polynesian Society in which the poem is published. In this note the outline of the story of the deceiving of Kewa is quite fully translated, and is substantially the same as "The Bride from the Under-world."

"The Deceiving of Kewa," as the New Zealand story is called, has this record among the Maoris. "This narrative is of old, of ancient times, very, very old. 'The Deceiving of Kewa' is an old, old story." Milu in some parts of the Pacific is the name of the place where the spirits of the dead dwell. Sometimes it is the name of the ruler of that place. In this ancient New Zealand legend it takes the place of Hiku, and is the name of the person who goes down into the depths after his bride, while the spirit-king is called Kewa, a part of the name Kewalu, which was the name of the Hawaiian bride whose ghost was brought back from the grave.

This, then, is the New Zealand legend, "The Deceiving of Kewa." There once lived in Hawaiki a chief and his wife. They had a child, a girl, born to them; then the mother died. The chief took another wife, who was not pleasing to the people. His anger was so great that the chief went away to the great forest of Tane (the god Kane in Hawaiian), and there built a house for himself and his wife.

After a time a son was born to them and the father named him Miru. This father was a great tohunga (kahuna), or

priest, as well as a chief. He taught Miru all the supreme
kinds of knowledge, all the invocations and incantations, those
for the stars, for the winds, for foods, for the sea, and for the
land. He taught him the peculiar incantations which would
enable him to meet all cunning tricks and enmities of man.
He learned also all the great powers of witchcraft. It is
said that on one occasion Miru and his father went to a river,
a great river. Here the child experimented with his powerful charms. He was a child of the forest and knew the
charm which could conquer the trees. Now there was a
tall tree growing by the side of the river. When Miru saw
it he recited his incantations. As he came to the end the
tree fell, the head reaching right across the river. They
left the tree lying in this way that it might be used as a
bridge by the people who came to the river. Thus he was
conscious of his power to correctly use the mighty invocations
which his father had taught him.

The years passed and the boy became a young man. His
was a lonely life, and he often wondered if there were not
those who could be his companions. At last he asked his
parents: "Are we here, all of us? Have I no other relative
in the world?"

His parents answered, "You have a sister, but she dwells
at a distant place."

When Miru heard this he arose and proceeded to search
for his sister, and he happily came to the very place where
she dwelt. There the young people were gathered in their
customary place for playing teka (Hawaiian keha). The
teka was a dart which was thrown along the ground, usually
the hard beach of the seashore. Miru watched the game for
some time and then returned to his home in the forest. He
told his father about the teka and the way it was played.
Then the chief prepared a teka for Miru, selected from the
best tree and fashioned while appropriate charms were
repeated.

Miru threw his dart along the slopes covered by the forest
and its underbrush, but the ground was uneven and the
undergrowth retarded the dart. Then Miru found a plain
and practised until he was very expert.

After a while he came to the place where his sister lived.
When the young people threw their darts he threw his. Aha!
it flew indeed and was lost in the distance. When the sister
beheld him she at once felt a great desire toward him.

The people tried to keep Miru with them, pleading with him to stay, and even following him as he returned to his forest home, but they caught him not. Frequently he repeated his visits, but never stayed long.

The sister, whose name is not given in the New Zealand legends, was disheartened, and hanged herself until she was dead. The body was laid in its place for the time of wailing. Miru and his father came to the uhunga, or place of mourning. The people had not known that Miru was the brother of the one who was dead. They welcomed the father and son according to their custom. Then the young man said, "After I leave, do not bury my sister." So the body was left in its place when the young man arose.

He went on his way till he saw a canoe floating. He then gave the command to his companions and they all paddled away in the canoe. They paddled on for a long distance, in fact to Rerenga-wai-rua, the point of land in New Zealand from which the spirits of the dead take their last leap as they go down to the Under-world. When they reached this place they rested, and Miru let go the anchor. He then said to his companions, "When you see the anchor rope shaking, pull it up, but wait here for me."

The young man then leaped into the water and went down, down near the bottom, and then entered a cave. This cave was the road by which the departed spirits went to spirit-land. Miru soon saw a house standing there. It was the home of Kewa, the chief of the Under-world. Within the house was his sister in spirit form.

Miru carried with him his nets which were given magic power, with which he hoped to catch the spirit of his sister. In many ways he endeavored to induce her ghost to come forth from the house of Kewa, but she would not come. He commenced whipping his top in the yard outside, but could not attract her attention. At last he set up a swing and many of the ghosts joined in the pastime. For a long time the sister remained within, but eventually came forth induced by the attraction of the swing and by the appearance of Miru. Miru then took the spirit in his arms and began to swing.

Higher and higher they rose whilst he incited the ghosts to increase to the utmost the flight of the moari, or swing. On reaching the highest point he gathered the spirit of the sister into his net, then letting go the swing away they flew and alighted quite outside the spirit-land.

Thence he went to the place where the anchor of the floating canoe was. Shaking the rope his friends understood the signal. He was drawn up with the ghost in his net. He entered the canoe and returned home. On arrival at the settlement the people were still lamenting. What was that to him? Taking the spirit he laid it on the dead body, at the same time reciting his incantations. The spirit gradually entered the body and the sister was alive again. This is the end of the narrative, but it is of old, of ancient times, very, very old. "The Deceiving of Kewa" is an old, old story.

In the Maori poem in which the reference to Kewa is made which brought out the above translation of one of the old New Zealand stories are also many other references to semi-historical characters and events. At the close of the poem is the following note: "The lament is so full of references to the ancient history of the Maoris that it would take a volume to explain them all. Most of the incidents referred to occurred in Hawaiki before the migration of the Maoris to New Zealand or at least five hundred to six hundred years ago."

Another New Zealand legend ought to be noticed in connection with the Hawaiian story of Hiku (Miru, New Zealand) seeking his sister in the Under-world. In what is probably the more complete Hawaiian story Hiku had a magic arrow which flew long distances and led him to the place where his sister-wife could be found.

In a New Zealand legend a magic dart leads a chief by the name of Tama in his search for his wife, who had been carried away to spirit-land. He threw the dart and followed it from place to place until he found a wrecked canoe, near which lay the body of his wife and her companions. He tried to bring her back to life, but his incantations were not strong enough to release the spirit.

Evidently the Hawaiian legend became a little fragmentary while being transplanted from the Hawaiian Islands to New Zealand. Hiku, the young chief who overcomes Miru of the spirit-world, loses his name entirely. Kewalu, the sister, also loses her name, a part of which, Kewa, is given to the ruler of the Under-world, and the magic dart is placed in the hands of Tama in an entirely distinct legend which still keeps the thought of the wife-seeker. There can scarcely be any question but that the original legend belongs to the Hawaiian Islands, and was carried to New Zealand in the days of the sea-rovers.

HOMELESS AND DESOLATE GHOSTS

The spirits of the dead, according to a summary of ancient Hawaiian statements, were divided into three classes, each class bearing the prefix "ao," which meant either the enlightened or instructed class, or simply a crowd or number of spirits grouped together.

The first class, the Ao-Kuewa, were the desolate and the homeless spirits who during their residence in the body had no friends and no property.

The second class was called the Ao-Aumakuas. These were the groups of ghost-gods or spirit-ancestors of the Hawaiians. They usually remained near their old home as helpful protectors of the family to which they belonged, and were worshipped by the family.

The third class was the Ao-o-Milu. Milu was the chief god of the Under-world throughout the greater part of Polynesia. Many times the Under-world itself bore the name of Milu. The Ao-o-Milu were the souls of the departed of both the preceding classes who had performed all tasks, passed all barriers, and found their proper place in the land of the king of ghosts.

The old Hawaiians never intelligently classified these departed spirits and sometimes mixed them together in inextricable confusion, but in the legends and remarks of early Hawaiian writers these three classes are roughly sketched. The desolate ghost had no right to call any place its home, to which it could come, over which it could watch, and around which it could hover. It had to go to the desolate parts of the islands or into a wilderness or forest.

The homeless ghost had no one to provide even the shadow of food for it. It had to go into the dark places and search for butterflies, spiders, and other insects. These were the ordinary food for all ghosts unless there were worshippers to place offerings on secret altars, which were often dedicated to gain a special power of praying other people to death. Such ghosts were well cared for, but, on the other hand, the desolate ones must wander and search until they could go down into the land of Milu.

There were several ways which the gods had prepared for

ghosts to use in this journey to the Under-world. It is interesting to note that all through Polynesia as well as in the
Hawaiian Islands the path for ghosts led westward.

The students of New Zealand folk-lore will say that this
signified the desire of those about to die to return to the land
of their ancestors beyond the western ocean.

The paths were called Leina-a-ka-uhane (paths-for-leaping-
by-the-spirit). They were almost always on bold bluffs
looking westward over the ocean. The spirit unless driven
back could come to the headland and leap down into the land
of the dead, but when this was done that spirit could never
return to the body it had left. Frequently connected with
these Leina-a-ka-uhane was a breadfruit-tree which would
be a gathering-place for ghosts.

At these places there were often friendly ghosts who
would help and sometimes return the spirit to the body or
send it to join the Ao-Aumakuas (ancestor ghosts). At the
place of descent it was said there was an owawa (ditch)
through which the ghosts one by one were carried down to
Po, and Lei-lono was the gate where the ghosts were killed
as they went down. Near this gateway was the Ulu-o-lei-
walo, or breadfruit-tree of the spirits. This tree had two
branches, one toward the east and one toward the west,
both of which were used by the ghosts. One was for leaping
into eternal darkness into Po-pau-ole, the other as a meeting-
place with the helpful gods.

This tree always bore the name Ulu-o-lei-walo (the-
quietly-calling-breadfruit-tree). On the island of Oahu,
one of these was said to have been at Kaena Point; another
was in Nuuanu Valley.

The desolate ghost would come to this meeting-place of
the dead and try to find a ghost of the second class, the
aumakuas, who had been one of his ancestors and who still
had some family to watch over. Perhaps this one might
entertain or help him.

If the ghost could find no one to take him, then he would
try to wander around the tree and leap into the branches.
The rotten, dead branches of the tree belonged to the spirits.
When they broke and fell, the spirits on them dropped into
the land of Milu—the under-world home of ghosts. Often
the spirit could leap from these dead branches into the Under-
world.

Sometimes the desolate spirit would be blown, as by the

wind, back and forth, here and there, until no possible place of rest could be found on the island where death had come; then the ghost would leap into the sea, hoping to find the way to Milu through some sea-cave. Perhaps the waves would carry the ghost, or it might be able to swim to one of the other islands, where a new search would be made for some ancestor-ghost from which to obtain help. Not finding aid, it would be pushed and driven over rough, rocky places and through the wilderness until it again went into the sea. At last perhaps a way would be found into the home of the dead, and the ghost would have a place in which to live, or it might make the round through the wilderness again and again, until it could leap from a bluff, or fall from a rotten branch of the breadfruit-tree.

A great caterpillar was the watchman on the eastern side of the leaping-off place. Napaha was the western boundary. A mo-o (dragon) was the watchman on that side. If the ghost was afraid of them it went back to secure the help of the ghost-gods in order to get by. The Hawaiians were afraid that these watchmen would kill ghosts if possible.

If a caterpillar obstructed the way it would raise its head over the edge of the bluff, and then the frightened ghost would go far out of its way, and wandering around be destroyed or compelled to leap off some dead branch into eternal darkness. But if that frightened ghost, while wandering, could find a helpful ghost god, it would be kept alive, although still a wanderer over the islands.

At the field of kaupea (coral) near Barbers Point, in the desert of Puuloa, the ghosts would go around among the lehua flowers, catching spiders, butterflies, and insects for food, where the ghost-gods might find them and give them aid in escaping the watchmen.

There are many places for the Leina-a-ka-uhane (leaping-off-places) and the Ulu-o-lei-walo (breadfruit-trees) on all the islands. To these places the wandering desolate ghosts went to find a way to the Under-world.

Another name for the wandering ghosts was lapu, also sometimes called Akua-hele-loa (great travellers). These ghosts were frequently those who enjoyed foolish, silly pranks. They would sweep over the old byways in troops, dancing and playing. They would gather around the old mats where the living had been feasting, and sit and feast on imaginary food.

The Hawaiians say: "On one side of the island Oahu, even to this day the lapu come at night. Their ghost drums and sacred chants can be heard and their misty forms seen as they hover about the ruins of the old heiaus (temples)."

The fine mists or fogs of Manoa Valley were supposed to conceal a large company of priests and their attendants while roaming among the great stones which still lie where there was a puu-honua (refuge-temple) in the early days. If any one saw these roving ghosts he was called lapu-ia, or one to whom spirits had appeared.

The Hawaiians said: "The lapu ghosts were not supposed to watch over the welfare of the persons they met. They never went into the heavens to become black clouds, bringing rain for the benefit of their households. They did not go out after winds to blow with destructive force against their enemies. This was the earnest work of the ancestor-ghosts, and was not done by the lapu."

Another name for ghosts was wai-lua, which referred especially to the spirit leaving the body and supposed to have been seen by some one. This wai-lua spirit could be driven back into the body by other ghosts, or persuaded to come back through offerings or incantations given by living friends, so that a dead person could become alive again.

It was firmly believed that a person could endure many deaths, and that if any one lost consciousness he was dead, and that when life stopped it was because the spirit left the body. When life was renewed it was because the spirit had returned to its former home.

The kino-wai-lua was a ghost leaving the body of a living person and returning after a time, as when any one fainted.

Besides the ghosts of the dead, the Hawaiians gave spirit power to all natural objects. Large stones were supposed to have dragon power sometimes.

AUMAKUAS, OR ANCESTOR-GHOSTS

There are two meanings to the first part of this word, for "au" means a multitude, as in "auwaa" (many canoes), but it may mean time and place, as in the following: "Our ancestors thought that if there was a desolate place where no man could be found, it was the aumakua (place of many gods)." "Makua" was the name given to the ancestors of a chief and of the people as well as to parents.

The aumakuas were the ghosts who did not go down into Po, the land of King Milu. They were in the land of the living, hovering around the families from which they had been separated by death. They were the guardians of these families.

When any one died, many devices were employed in disposing of the body. The fact that an enemy of the family might endeavor to secure the bones of the dead for the purpose of making them into fish-hooks, arrow-heads, or spear-heads led the surviving members of a family either to destroy or to conceal the body of the dead. For if the bones were so used it meant great dishonor, and the spirit was supposed to suffer on account of this indignity.

Sometimes the flesh was stripped from the bones and cast into the ocean or into the fires of the volcanoes, that the ghost might be made a part of the family ghosts who lived in such places, and the bones were buried in some secret cave or pit, or folded together in a bundle, and these were called unihipili. The unihipili bones were used in connection with a strange belief called pule-ana-ana (praying to death).

When the body of a dead person was to be hidden, only two or three men were employed in the task. Sometimes the one highest in rank would slay his helpers so that no one except himself would know the burial-place.

The tools, the clothing, and the calabashes of the dead were unclean until certain ceremonies of purification had been faithfully performed. Many times these possessions were either placed in the burial-cave beside the body or burned so that they might be the property of the spirit in ghost-land.

The people who cared for the body had to bathe in sa. water and separate themselves from the family for a time. They must sprinkle the house and all things inside with salt water. After a few days the family would return and occupy the house once more.

Usually the caretakers of a dead body would make a hole in the side of the house and push it through rather than take it through the old doorway, probably having the idea that the ghost would only know the door through which the body had gone out when alive and so could not find the new way back when the opening was closed.

After death came, the ghost crept out of the body, coming up from the feet until it rested in the eyes, and then it came out from the corner of one eye, and had a kind of wind body. It could pass around the room and out of doors through any opening it could find. It could perch like a bird on the roof of a house or in the branches of trees, or it could seat itself on logs or stones near the house. It might have to go back into the body and make it live again. Possibly the ghost might meet some old ancestor-ghosts and be led so far away that it could not return; then it must become a member of the aumakua, or ancestor-ghost, family, or wander off to join the homeless desolate ghost vagabonds.

Sometimes dead bodies were thrown into the sea with the hope that the ghost body would become a shark or an eel, or perhaps a mo-o, or dragon-god, to be worshipped with other ancestor-gods of the same class.

Sometimes the body or the bones would be cast into the crater of Kilauea, the people thinking the spirit would become a flame of fire like Pele, the goddess of volcanoes; other spirits went into the air concealed in the dark depths of the sky, perhaps in the clouds.

Here they carried on the work needed to help their families. They would become fog or mist or the fine misty rain colored by light. With these the Rainbow Maiden, Anuenue, delighted to dwell. They often lived in the great rolling white clouds, or in the gray clouds which let fall the quiet rain needed for farming. They also lived in the fierce black thunder-clouds which sent down floods of a devastating character upon the enemies of the family to which they belonged.

There were ghost ancestors who made their homes near the places where the members of their families toiled; there were ancestor-ghosts to take care of the tapa, or kapa, makers, or the calabash or house or canoe makers. There were special ancestor-ghosts called upon by name by the farmers, the fishermen, and the bird-hunters. These ghosts had their own kuleanaș, or places to which they belonged, and in which they had their own peculiar duties and privileges. They became ancestor ghost-gods and dwelt on the islands near the homes of their worshippers, or in the air above, or in the trees around the houses, or in the ocean or in the glowing fires of volcanoes. They even dwelt in human beings, making them shake or sneeze as with cold, and then a person was said to become an ipu, or calabash containing a ghost.

Sometimes it was thought that a ghost-god could be seen sitting on the head or shoulder of the person to whom it belonged. Even in this twentieth century a native woman told the writer that she saw a ghost-god whispering in his ear while he was making an address. She said, "That ghost was like a fire or a colored light." Many times the Hawaiians have testified that they believed in the presence of their ancestor ghost-gods.

This is the way the presence of a ghost was detected: Some sound would be heard, such as a sibilant noise, a soft whistle, or something like murmurs, or some sensation in a part of the body might be felt. If an eyelid trembled, a ghost was sitting on that spot. A quivering or creepy feeling in any part of the body meant that a ghost was touching that place. If any of these things happened, a person would cry out, "I have seen or felt a spirit of the gods."

Sometimes people thought they saw the spirits of their ghost friends. They believed that the spirits of these friends appeared in the night, sometimes to kill any one who was in the way. The high chiefs and warriors are supposed to march and go in crowds, carrying their spears and piercing those they met unless some ghost recognized that one and called to the others, "Alia [wait]," but if the word was "O-i-o [throw the spear]!" then that spirit's spear would strike death to the passer-by.

There were night noises which the natives attributed to sounds or rustling motions made by such night gods as the following:

Akua-hokio (whistling gods).
   " -kiei (peeping gods).
   " -nalo (prying gods).
   " -loa (long gods).
   " -poko (short gods).
   " -muki (sibilant gods).

A prayer to these read thus:

"O Akua-loa! [long god]
O Akua-poko! [short god]
O Akua-muki! [god breathing in short, sibilant breaths
O Akua-hokio! [god blowing like whistling winds]
O Akua-kiei! [god watching, peeping at one]
O Akua-nalo! [god hiding, slipping out of sight]
O All ye Gods, who travel on the dark night paths!
Come and eat.
Give life to me,
And my parents,
And my children,
To us who are living in this place.   Amama [Amen]."

This prayer was offered every night as a protection against
the ghosts.

The aumakuas were very laka (tame and helpful). It was
said that an aumakua living in a shark would be very laka,
and would come to be rubbed on the head, opening his mouth
for a sacrifice. Perhaps some awa, or meat, would be placed
in his mouth, and then he would go away. So also if the aumakua were a bird, it would become tame. If it were the
alae (a small duck), it would come to the hand of its worshipper; if the pueo (owl), it would come and scratch the
earth away from the grave of one of its worshippers, throwing
the sand away with its wings, and would bring the body
back to life. An owl ancestor-god would come and set a
worshipper free were he a prisoner with hands and feet bound
by ropes.

It made no difference whether the dead person were male
or female, child or aged one, the spirit could become a ghost-
god and watch over the family.

There were altars for the ancestor-gods in almost every land.
These were frequently only little piles of white coral, but
sometimes chiefs would build a small house for their ancestor-
gods, thus making homes that the ghosts might have a kuleana,
or place of their own, where offerings could be placed, and
prayers offered, and rest enjoyed.

The Hawaiians have this to say about sacrifices for the
aumakuas: If a mo-o, or dragon-god, was angry with its
caretaker or his family and they became weak and sick,
they would sacrifice a spotted dog with awa, red fish, red
sugar-cane, and some of the grass growing in taro patches
wrapped in yellow kapa. This they would take to the lua,
or hole, where the mo-o dwelt, and fasten the bundle there.
Then the mo-o would become pleasant and take away the

sickness. If it were a shark-god, the sacrifice was a black pig, a dark red chicken, and some awa wrapped in new white kapa made by a virgin. This bundle would be carried to the beach, where a prayer would be offered:

> "O aumakuas from sunrise to sunset,
> From North to South, from above and below,
> O spirits of the precipice and spirits of the sea,
> All who dwell in flowing waters,
> Here is a sacrifice—our gifts are to you.
> Bring life to us, to all the family,
> To the old people with wrinkled skin,
> To the young also.
> This is our life,
> From the gods."

Then the farmer would throw the bundle into the sea, bury the chicken alive, take the pig to the temple, then go back to his house looking for rain. If there was rain, it showed that the aumakua had seen the gifts and washed away the wrong. If the clouds became black with heavy rain, that was well.

The offerings for Pele and Hiiaka were awa to drink and food to eat, in fact all things which could be taken to the crater.

This applies to the four great gods, Kane, Ku, Lono, and Kanaloa. They are called the first of the ancestors. Each one of these was supposed to be able to appear in a number of different forms, therefore each had a number of names expressive of the work he intended or was desired to do. An explanatory adjective or phrase was added to the god's own name, defining certain acts or characteristics, thus: Kane-puaa (Kane, the pig) was Kane who would aid in stirring up the ground like a pig.

This is one of the prayers used when presenting offerings to aumakuas, "O Aumakuas of the rising of the sun, guarded by every tabu staff, here are offerings and sacrifices—the black pig, the white chicken, the black cocoanut, the red fish—sacrifices for the gods and all the aumakuas; those of the ancestors, those of the night, and of the dawn, here am I. Let life come."

The ancestor-gods were supposed to use whatever object they lived with. If ghosts went up into the clouds, they moved the clouds from place to place and made them assume such shapes as might be fancied. Thus they would reveal themselves over their old homes.

All the aumakuas were supposed to be gentle and ready to help their own families. The old Hawaiians say that the power of the ancestor-gods was very great. "Here is the magic power. Suppose a man would call his shark, 'O Kuhai-moana [the shark-god]! O, the One who lives in the Ocean! Take me to the land!' Then perhaps a shark would appear, and the man would get on the back of the shark, hold fast to the fin, and say: 'You look ahead. Go on very swiftly without waiting.' Then the shark would swim swiftly to the shore."

The old Hawaiians had the sport called "lua." This sometimes meant wrestling, but usually was the game of catching a man, lifting him up, and breaking his body so that he was killed. A wrestler of the lua class would go out to a plain where no people were dwelling and call his god Kuialua. The aumakua ghost-god would give this man strength and skill, and help him to kill his adversaries.

There were many priests of different classes who prayed to the ancestor-gods. Those of the farmers prayed like this:

> "O great black cloud in the far-off sky,
> O shadow watching shadow,
> Watch over our land.
> Overshadow our land
> From corner to corner
> From side to side.
> Do not cast your shadow on other lands
> Nor let the waters fall on the other lands
> [*i.e.*, keep the rains over my place]."

Also they prayed to Kane-puaa (Kane, the pig), the great aumakua of farmers:

> "O Kane-puaa, root!
> Dig inland, dig toward the sea;
> Dig from corner to corner,
> From side to side;
> Let the food grow in the middle,
> Potatoes on the side roots,
> Fruit in the centre.
> Do not root in another place!
> The people may strike you with the spade [o-o]
> Or hit you with a stone
> And hurt you. Amama [Amen]."

So also they prayed to Kukea-olo-walu (a taro aumakua god):

> "O Kukea-olo-walu!
> Make the taro grow.
> Let the leaf spread like a banana.
> Taro for us, O Kukea!
> The banana and the taro for us.
> Puli up the taro for us, O Kukea!
> Pound the taro.

Make the fire for cooking the pig.
Give life to us—
To the farmers—
From sunrise to sunset
From one fastened place to the other fastened place
[*i.e.*, one side of the sky to the other fastened on each side of the earth]. Amama [Amen]."

Trees with their branches and fruit were frequently endowed with spirit power. All the different kinds of birds and even insects, and also the clouds and winds and the fish in the seas were given a place among the spirits around the Hawaiians.

The people believed in life and its many forms of power. They would pray to the unseen forces for life for themselves and their friends, and for death to come on the families of their enemies. They had special priests and incantations for the pule-ana-ana, or praying to death, and even to the present time the supposed power to pray to death is one of the most formidable terrors to their imagination.

Menehunes, eepas, and kupuas were classes of fairies or gnomes which did not belong to the ancestor-gods, or aumakuas.

The menehunes were fairy servants. Some of the Polynesian Islands called the lowest class of servants "manahune." The Hawaiians separated them almost entirely from the spirits of ancestors. They worked at night performing prodigious tasks which they were never supposed to touch again after the coming of dawn.

The eepas were usually deformed and defective gnomes. They suffered from all kinds of weakness, sometimes having no bones and no more power to stand than a large leaf. They were sometimes set apart as spirit caretakers of little children. Nuuanu Valley was the home of a multitude of eepas who had their temple on the western side of the valley.

Kupuas were the demons of ghost-land. They were very powerful and very destructive. No human being could withstand their attacks unless specially endowed with power from the gods. They had animal as well as human bodies and could use whichever body seemed to be most available. The dragons, or mo-os, were the most terrible kupuas in the islands.

THE DRAGON GHOST–GODS

Dragons were among the ghost-gods of the ancient
Hawaiians. These dragons were called mo-o. The New
Zealanders used the same names for some of their large reptile
gods. They, however, spelled the word with a "k," calling
it mo-ko, and it was almost identical in pronunciation as in
meaning with the Hawaiian name. Both the Hawaiians
and New Zealanders called all kinds of lizards mo-o or mo-ko;
and their use of this word in traditions showed that they
often had in mind animals like crocodiles and alligators, and
sometimes they referred the name to any monster of great
mythical powers belonging to a man-destroying class.

Mighty eels, immense sea-turtles, large fish of the ocean,
fierce sharks, were all called mo-o. The most ancient dragons
of the Hawaiians are spoken of as living in pools or lakes.
These dragons were known also as kupuas, or mysterious
characters who could appear as animals or human beings
according to their wish. The saying was: "Kupuas have a
strange double body."

There were many other kupuas besides those of the dragon
family. It was sometimes thought that at birth another
natural form was added, such as an egg of a fowl or a bird,
or the seed of a plant, or the embryo of some animal, which
when fully developed made a form which could be used as
readily as the human body. These kupuas were always
given some great magic power. They were wonderfully
strong and wise and skilful.

Usually the birth of a kupua, like the birth of a high chief,
was attended with strange disturbances in the heavens, such
as reverberating thunder, flashing lightning, and severe
storms which sent the abundant red soil of the islands down
the mountain-sides in blood-red torrents known as ka-ua-koko
(the blood rain). This name was also given to misty fine rain
when shot through by the red waves of the sun.

By far the largest class of kupuas was that of the dragons.
These all belonged to one family. Their ancestor was Mo-o-
inanea (The Self-reliant Dragon), who figured very promi-
nently in the Hawaiian legends of the most ancient times,
such as "The Maiden of the Golden Cloud."

Mo-o-inanea (The Self-reliant Dragon) brought the dragons, the kupua dragons, from the "Hidden Land of Kane" to the Hawaiian Islands. Mo-o-inanea was apparently a demi-goddess of higher power even than the gods Ku, Kane, or Kanaloa. She was the great dragon-goddess of the Hawaiians, coming to the islands in the migration of the gods from Nuu-mea-lani and Kuai-he-lani to settle. The dragons and other kupuas came as spirit servants of the gods.

For a while this Mo-o-inanea lived with her brothers, the gods, at Waolani, but after a long time there were so many dragons that it was necessary to distribute them over the islands, and Mo-o-inanea decided to leave her brothers and find homes for her numerous family. So she went down to Puunui in the lower part of Nuuanu Valley and there made her home, and it is said received worship from the men of the ancient days. Here she dwelt in her dual nature— sometimes appearing as a dragon, sometimes as a woman.

Very rich clayey soil was found in this place, forced out of the earth as if by geyser action. It was greatly sought in later years by the chiefs who worshipped this goddess. They made the place tabu, and used the clay, sometimes eating it, but generally plastering the hair with it. This place was made very tabu by the late Queen Kaahumanu during her lifetime.

Mo-o-inanea lived in the pit from which this clay was procured, a place called Lua-palolo, meaning pit-of-sticky-clay. After she had come to this dwelling-place the dragons were sent out to find homes. Some became chiefs and others servants, and when by themselves were known as the evil ones. She distributed her family over all the islands from Hawaii to Niihau. Two of these dragon-women, according to the legends, lived as guardians of the pali (precipice) at the end of Nuuanu Valley, above Honolulu. After many years it was supposed that they both assumed the permanent forms of large stones which have never lost their associations with mysterious, miraculous power.

Even as late as 1825, Mr. Bloxam, the chaplain of the English man-of-war, recorded in "The Voyage of the Blonde" the following statement:

"At the bottom of the Parre (pali) there are two large stones on which even now offerings of fruits and flowers are laid to propitiate the Aku-wahines, or goddesses, who are supposed to have the power of granting a safe passage."

Mr. Bloxam says that these were a kind of mo-o, or reptile, goddesses, and adds that it was difficult to explain the meaning of the name given to them, probably because the Hawaiians had nothing in the shape of serpents or large reptiles in their islands.

A native account of these stones says: "There is a large grove of hau-trees in Nuuanu Valley, and above these lie the two forest women, Hau-ola and Ha-puu. These are now two large stones, one being about three feet long with a fine smooth back, the other round with some little rough places. The long stone is on the seaward side, and this is the Mo-o woman, Hau-ola; and the other, Ha-puu. The leaves of ferns cover Hau-ola, being laid on that stone. On the other stone, Ha-puu, are lehua flowers. These are kupuas."

Again the old people said that their ancestors had been accustomed to bring the navel cords of their children and bury them under these stones to insure protection of the little ones from evil, and that these were the stone women of Nuuanu.

Ala-muki lived in the deep pools of the Waialua River near the place Ka-mo-o-loa, which received its name from the long journeys that dragon made over the plains of Waialua. She and her descendants guarded the paths and sometimes destroyed those who travelled that way.

One dragon lived in the Ewa lagoon, now known as Pearl Harbor. This was Kane-kua-ana, who was said to have brought the pipi (oysters) to Ewa. She was worshipped by those who gathered the shell-fish. When the oysters began to disappear about 1850, the natives said that the dragon had become angry and was sending the oysters to Kahiki, or some far-away foreign land.

Kilioe, Koe, and Milolii were noted dragons on the island of Kauai. They were the dragons of the precipices of the northern coast of this island, who took the body of the high chief Lohiau and concealed it in a cave far up the steep side of the mountain. There is a very long interesting story of the love between Lohiau and Pele, the goddess of fire. In this story Pele overcame the dragons and won the love of the chief. Hiiaka, the sister of the fire-goddess, won a second victory over them when she rescued a body from the cave and brought it back to life.

On Maui, the greatest dragon of the island was Kiha-wahine. The natives had the saying, "Kiha has mana, or miraculous power, like Mo-o-inanea." She lived in a large deep pool on the edge of the village Lahaina, and was worshipped by the royal family of Maui as their special guardian.

There were many dragons of the island of Hawaii, and the most noted of these were the two who lived in the Wailuku River near Hilo. They were called "the moving boards" which made a bridge across the river.

Sometimes they accepted offerings and permitted a safe passage, and sometimes they tipped the passengers into the water and drowned them. They were destroyed by Hiiaka.

Sacred to these dragons who were scattered over all the islands were the mo-o priests and the sorcerers, who propitiated them with offerings and sacrifices, chanting incantations.

THE HOME OF THE ANCESTORS

The ancestors of the New Zealand Maoris have a definite ancestral home from which they came to New Zealand. This bears the name Hawaiki, which is the same as Hawai'i as also Savai'i in Samoa. Some students try to make Samoa the distributing centre from which the settlers of the various island groups of the Pacific started to find new homes. This theory has scarcely any foundation.

Hawaii in some form of the word is found from Java on the western side of the Pacific to Tahiti on the eastern. Hon. L. Percy Smith of New Zealand says: "The universality of this name points to the fact that it is extremely ancient and that it was under that form the Fatherland was originally known. The way in which the name has been used proves the belief of the Polynesians in a western origin of the race now accepted as from India. Hawa in its many forms refers to rice fields, the great rice fields of Indonesia."

While Hawaii is used so frequently elsewhere, it is seldom named in the Hawaiian Islands as the ancestral home. Fornander, in "The Polynesian Race," quotes from an ancient chant, "Hawaii with the green back and dotted sea," and says this refers to the ancient far-away home of the Hawaiians. This reference stands almost alone, and therefore emphasizes the statement that the word Hawaiian seldom refers to any land outside the group now called the Hawaiian Islands. This has probably come from the inability of the people to distinguish between a foreign Hawaii and a home Hawaii, although for centuries they have said "Hawaii nei," meaning "the Hawaii in this spot," as they say "hale nei," meaning "this particular house in which we are." Almost certainly this has no reference to an ancestral home.

The Hawaiians, however, had one word for all outside lands. This was Kahiki or Tahiti. If any one sailed to any far-away place, east or west, he went to Kahiki.

The ancient Hawaiian chants also mention places or rather islands in the western and southwestern parts of the Pacific Ocean, as Bolabola, Nuuhiwa, Wawau or Vavau, and Upolu. These places were visited by the Hawaiian sea-rovers several hundred years ago and the names preserved in meles, or chants. Usually these places are mentioned as located in the great mysterious outside world Kahiki. They are not called the home from which the forefathers came. They are only definite places visited by sea-roving Hawaiians in their long journeys to foreign lands.

Besides this, there were some beautiful descriptive terms naming the ancestral islands or lands from which the "ancient ones came to Hawaii."

The most prominent was Kuai-he-lani or Kua-i-he-lani. Kuai-he-lani was defined by one of the best Hawaiian scholars as "the purchased heaven." This, however, is a modern thought, read into it from theology. Another and better rendering is "the rubbing or grinding heaven," as if the land had been stirred up by earthquakes or by strife among the inhabitants. If the name is Kua-i-he-lani, it means "a heaven lifted up in sharp ridges," signifying that the people came from a land of high mountains with sharp peaks, a volcanic country.

Kane-huna-moku (the hidden land of Kane) belonged more to the spirit world than the home of the ancestors. It was like an "ignis fatuus," a thing which appeared and disappeared. It was an enticing island, inviting boatmen to seek its shores and then disappearing as they came near. It was the Hawaiian dreamland. Nevertheless, sometimes it was mentioned as one of the places from which the ancestors came.

Nuu-mea-lani (the raised dais of heaven), meaning a land with elevated plateaus and possibly rich valleys among high mountains, was a place from which many of the people of the past came to the new volcano land. Sometimes it simply means "cloud land."

Ulu-kaa (moving or floating forest) was, like Kane-huna-moku, an ocean island which had no abiding place. Storm-driven voyagers would see it through the mist clouds around them. They would put forth every effort to reach it and never find it, or, if found, its sweet fruits and fragrant flowers were like dust to those who ate or breathed them, ultimately bringing death. Nevertheless, Ulu-kaa was a land from which the ancestors came.

Hapa-kuela is very seldom mentioned in the legends. Its meaning is very obscure. It is possible that it may be Hapaku-wela. Then it might mean the burning or fiery portions or walls between land districts. This was a home of

Pele according to some of the Hawaiian legends, although most of them say that she came from Kuai-he-lani.

Ke-alohi-lani (the shining or glorious heaven) was the land where the vivid imagination placed all things beautiful. It was the ancient land to be desired. Another interpretation, however, makes it the land of shining clouds, probably lit up by volcanic fires, reflecting the glory of the burning flames.

Moku-mana-mana (the divided island) was some island projecting into the ocean like branches from a tree, an island with bays and inlets. This was one of the places to be desired among the different lands from which the ancestors came. Now it is only known as one of the ancestral places lying toward the sunset.

APPENDIX

HONOLULU AQUARIUM

The Honolulu Aquarium is located in Kapiolani Park on the famous Waikiki Beach, about five miles from the centre of the city. From 600 to 1,000 fish, covering some 200 varieties of remarkable form and bewildering color, are on exhibition here, forming one of the finest collections in the world.

This Aquarium was built in 1904 by Mr. and Mrs. Chas. M. Cooke on land donated for the purpose by Mr. Jas. B. Castle, brother-in-law to Mr. Westervelt, the author, and is stocked and maintained by the Honolulu Rapid Transit Company. The plant has cost over $20.000, and is being added to and improved from time to time. The color plates included in this volume show only a few of these wonderful fish.

BISHOP MUSEUM

Mr. Chas. R. Bishop, who founded the Bishop Museum, died in California early in 1915, having just passed his ninety-third birthday. He was born in Glens Falls, N.Y., and sailed around Cape Horn to Hawaii in the early days before steam-ship communication.

His wife, Berenice Pauahi, was a very high chiefess descended from the royal line of Kamehameha the Great. To her Kamehameha V. offered the throne, and on her refusal to espouse him remained a bachelor and died without heir. Mrs. Pauahi Bishop bequeathed her vast estate and fortune to found the schools for Hawaiian boys and girls, known as the Kamehameha Schools, Honolulu, and near these Mr. Bishop founded the Bishop Museum; which contains all the magnificent feather-cloaks, helmets, calabashes, etc., handed down from generation to generation through the royal line of the Kamehamehas and inherited by Mrs. Bishop. This has been greatly increased by other gifts and purchases and now forms the finest museum in the world, of relics of the Polynesian race.

MELES

"The history of Hawaii can be traced only through the ancient meles, poems without rhyme or metre, but strictly accented, often several hundred lines in length, handed down orally from one generation to another. The mele included all forms of poetical composition intended for chanting. They are usually divided into four groups, as the religious chants, prayers, and prophecies; the inoas, or name songs composed at birth of a chief recounting heroic deeds of his ancestors; the kanikaus, or dirges for the dead; the ipos, or love songs.—All the modern songs are love songs.—The cadencing consisted of a prolonged trilling or fluctuating movement called *i-i*, in which the voice went up and down in an interval less than a half-tone. This was used extensively in the oli (a songful expression of joy, or a humorous narrative), which was even more lyric than the mele.

HULA

The modern hula is not the hula of ancient time. The hula combined pantomime, poetry, music, and the dance. It was enacted in honor of the goddess Laka and furnished entertainment for the chiefs and their retinues. It included the mysteries of Polynesian mythology and the history of the nation. It was given by trained and paid performers, as it was a difficult accomplishment and required long and rigid training in both song and dance.

Hulas varied in dignity and rank, and the character was influenced by the musical instruments used, which were as follows: the ipu, a drum made of two large pear-shaped gourds of unequal size, joined together at the smaller ends, in which a hole was made to increase the resonance; the pahu, a drum made of coconut wood and covered with shark skin on its upper end, originally used in the heiaus and on rare occasions in the halau; the puniu used with the pahu, a small drum made from a coconut shell and fish skin, which was strapped to the thigh and played with a thong of braided fibres; the uli uli, a small gourd filled with seeds; the puili, bamboo sticks splintered into fine divisions at one end and giving a rustling sound like wind; the laau, two pieces of resonant wood; the ili ili, two pebbles used like castanets; the ukeke, something like a jew's-harp—the strings being plucked with ribs of grass; the conch shell, or trumpet; the pua, a small gourd; and the ohe, or nose flute.

The ukelele, a small guitar having only four strings, now used was introduced in the time of Kalakaua and is modern. It affords, however, an effective accompaniment for the deep, rich quality of the Hawaiian voices.

The halau was a flat-topped open structure covered usually with coconut leaves specially erected for the performance of the hula and to which leis and awa were brought as emblems of light-heartedness and joy. In every halau there was a bower of green leaves which were supposed to be the abode of the presiding deity. The devotees of the hula worshipped many gods, but the goddess Laka was the patron to whom special prayers and offerings were made."

(Excerpt from an article by Helen G. Cadwell.—*Thrum's Annual*, 1916.)

PARTIAL LIST OF HAWAIIAN TERMS USED

POLYNESIAN LANGUAGE

"A few words should be added on the peculiar genius and structure of the Polynesian language in general and of the Hawaïan dialect in particular.

It is the law of all Polynesian languages that every word and syllable must end in a vowel, so that no two consonants are ever heard without a vowel sound between them.

Most of the radical words are dissyllables, and the accent is generally on the penult. The Polynesian ear is as nice in marking the slightest variations in vowel sound as it is dull in distinguishing consonants.

The vocabulary of the Hawaiian is probably richer than that of most other Polynesian tongues. Its child-like and primitive character is shown by the absence of abstract words and general terms.

As has been well observed by M. Gaussin, there are three classes of words, corresponding to as many different stages of language: first, those that express sensations; second, images; third, abstract ideas.

Not only are names wanting for the more general abstractions, such as space, nature, fate, etc., but there are very few generic terms. For example there is no generic term for animal, expressing the whole class of living creatures or for insects or for colors. At the same time it abounds in specific names and in nice distinctions.

So in the Hawaiian everything that relates to their every-day life or to the natural objects with which they are conversant is expressed with a vivacity, a minuteness and nicety of coloring which cannot be reproduced in a foreign tongue. Thus the Hawaiian was very rich in terms for every variety of cloud. It has names for every species of plant on the mountains or fish in the sea, and is peculiarly copious in terms relating to the ocean, the surf and waves.

For whatever belonged to their religions, their handicrafts or their amusements, their vocabulary was most copious and minute. Almost every stick in a native house had its appropriate name. Hence it abounds in synonyms which are such only in appearance, *i.e.*, "to be broken" as a stick is 'haki,' as a string is 'moku,' as a dish 'naha,' as a wall 'hina.'

Besides the language of every-day life, there was a style appropriate to oratory and another to religion and poetry.

The above-mentioned characteristics make it a pictorial and expressive language. It still has the freshness of childhood. Its words are pictures rather than colorless and abstract symbols of ideas, and are redolent of the mountain, the forest and the surf.

However it has been and is successfully used to express the abstractions of mathematics, of English law, and of theology."

"The Hawaiian is but a dialect of the great Polynesian language, which is spoken with extraordinary uniformity over all the numerous islands of the Pacific Ocean between New Zealand and Hawaii. Again, the Polynesian language is but one member of that wide-spread family of languages, known as the Malayo-Polynesian or Oceanic family, which extends from Madagascar to the Hawaiian Islands and from New Zealand to Formosa. The Hawaiian dialect is peculiarly interesting to the philologist from its isolated position, being the most remote of the family from its primeval seat in Southeastern Asia, and leading the van with the Malagasy in the rear. We believe the Hawaiian to be the most copious and expressive, as well as the richest in native traditional history and poetry. Dr. Reinhold Forster, the celebrated naturalist of Captain Cook's second voyage, drew up a table containing 47 words taken from 11 Oceanic dialects and the corresponding terms in Malay, Mexican, Peruvian and Chilian. From this table he inferred that the Polynesian languages afford many analogies with the Malay while they present no point of contact with the American.

Baron William von Humboldt, the distinguished statesman and scholar, showed that the Tagala, the leading language of the Philippine Islands, is by far the richest and most perfect of these languages. 'It possesses,' he says, 'all the forms collectively of which particular ones are found singly in other dialects; and it has preserved them all with very trifling exceptions unbroken and in entire harmony and symmetry.'

The languages of the Oceanic region have been divided into six great groups; *i.e.,* the Polynesian; the Micronesian; the Melanesian or Papuan; the Australian; the Malaysian; the Malagasy. Many examples might be given if they were needed to illustrate the connection of these languages. The Polynesian is an ancient and primitive member of the Malay family. The New Zealand dialect is the most primitive and entire in its forms. The Hawaiians, Marquesans and Tahitians form a closely related group by themselves. For example, the Marquesan converts are using Hawaiian books and the people of the Austral Islands read the Tahitian Bible."

The above was written by W. D. Alexander in Honolulu in 1865, author of the "History of the Hawaiian Islands" as preface to Andrew's Dictionary.

TALES OF THE PACIFIC

HAWAII

Ancient History of the Hawaiian People by Abraham Fornander
A reprint of this classic of precontact history tracing Hawaii's saga from legendary times to the arrival of Captain Cook, including an account of his demise. Originally published as volume II in *An Account of the Polynesian Race: Its Origins and Migration,* this historical work is an excellent reference for students and general readers alike. Written over a hundred years ago, it still represents one of the few compendiums of precontact history available in a single source.
$7.95   ISBN 1-56647-147-8

Hawaii: Fiftieth Star by A. Grove Day
Told for the junior reader, this brief history of America's fiftieth state should also beguile the concerned adult. "Interesting, enlightening, and timely reading for high school American and World History groups."
$4.95   ISBN 0-935180-44-3

A Hawaiian Reader
Thirty-seven selections from the literature of the past hundred years, including such writers as Mark Twain, Robert Louis Stevenson and James Jones.
$5.95   ISBN 0-935180-07-9

Hawaii and Its People by A. Grove Day
An informal, one-volume narrative of the exotic and fascinating history of the peopling of the archipelago. The periods range from the first arrivals of Polynesian canoe voyagers to attainment of American statehood. A "headline history" brings the story from 1960 to 1990.
$4.95   ISBN 0-935180-50-8

True Tales of Hawaii and the South Seas Edited by A. Grove Day and Carl Stroven
Yarns from the real Pacific by 21 master storytellers, including Mark Twain, W. Somerset Maugham, Robert Louis Stevenson, and James A. Michener. This anthology comprises some of the best nonfiction writing about the South Pacific.
$5.95   ISBN 0-935180-22-2

A Hawaiian Reader, Vol. II
A companion volume to *A Hawaiian Reader*. Twenty-four
selections from the exotic literary heritage of the Islands.
$6.95   ISBN 1-56647-207-5

Kona by Marjorie Sinclair
The best woman novelist of post-war Hawai'i dramatizes the
conflict between a daughter of Old Hawai'i and her straitlaced
Yankee husband. Nor is the drama resolved in their children.
$4.95   ISBN 0-935180-20-6

The Wild Wind, a novel by Marjorie Sinclair
On the Hana Coast of Maui, Lucia Gray, great-granddaughter
of a New England missionary, seeks solitude but embarks on
an interracial marriage with an Hawaiian cowboy. Then she
faces some of the mysteries of the Polynesia of old.
$5.95   ISBN 0-935180-3-3

Claus Spreckels, The Sugar King in Hawaii by Jacob Adler
Sugar was the main economic game in Hawai'i a century ago,
and the boldest player was Claus Spreckels, a California tycoon
who built a second empire in the Islands by ruthless and often
dubious means.
$5.95   ISBN 0-935180-76-1

Remember Pearl Harbor! by Blake Clark
An up-to-date edition of the first full-length account of the
effect of the December 7, 1941 "blitz" that precipitated
America's entrance into World War II and is still remembered
vividly by military and civilian survivors of the airborne
Japanese holocaust.
$4.95   ISBN 0-935180-49-4

Russian Flag Over Hawaii: The Mission of Jeffery Tolamy, a
novel by Darwin Teilhet
A vigorous adventure novel in which a young American strug-
gles to unshackle the grip held by Russian filibusters on the
Kingdom of Kauai. Kamehameha the Great and many other
historical figures play their roles in a colorful love story.
$5.95   ISBN 0-935180-28-1

Rape in Paradise by Theon Wright
The sensational "Massie Case" of the 1930's shattered the tranquil image that mainland U.S.A. had of Hawaii. One woman
shouted "Rape!" and the island erupted with such turmoil that
for 20 years it was deemed unprepared for statehood. A fascinating case study of race relations and military-civilian relations.
$5.95   ISBN 0-935180-88-5

Mark Twain in Hawaii: Roughing It in the Sandwich Islands
The noted humorist's account of his 1866 trip to Hawai'i at a time when the Islands were more for the native than the tourists. The writings first appeared in their present form in Twain's important book, *Roughing It.* Includes an introductory essay from *Mad About Islands* by A. Grove Day.
$4.95   ISBN 0-935180-93-1

The Trembling of a Leaf by W. Somerset Maugham
Stories of Hawai'i and the South Seas, including *Red,* the author's most successful story, and *Rain,* his most notorious one.
$4.95   ISBN 0-935180-21-4

Hawaii and Points South by A. Grove Day
Foreword by James A. Michener
A collection of the best of A. Grove Day's many shorter writings over a span of 40 years. The author has appended personal headnotes, revealing his reasons for choosing each particular subject.
$4.95   ISBN 0-935180-01-X

Pearl, a novel by Stirling Silliphant
In a world on the brink of war, the Hawaiian island of Oahu was still the perfect paradise. And in this lush and tranquil Pacific haven everyone clung to the illusion that their spectacular island could never be touched by the death and destruction of Hirohito's military machine.
$5.95   ISBN 0-935180-91-5

Horror in Paradise: Grim and Uncanny Tales from Hawaii and the South Seas, edited by A. Grove Day and Bacil F. Kirtley
Thirty-four writers narrate "true" episodes of sorcery and the supernatural, as well as gory events on sea and atoll.
$6.95   ISBN 0-935180-23-0

How to Order

For book rate (4-6 wekks; in Hawaii, 1-2 weeks)
send check or money order with an additional $3.00
for the first book and $1.00 for each additional book.
For fiirst class (1-2 weeks) add $4.00 for the first book, $3.00 for each
additional book.

1215 Center Street, Suite 210
Honolulu, HI 96816
Tel (808) 732-1709 Fax (808) 734-4094
Email: mutual@lava.net